HOW *NOT* TO EAT ULTRA-PROCESSED

T0322116

HOW *NOT* TO EAT ULTRA-PROCESSED

YOUR 4-WEEK PLAN FOR LIFE-CHANGING HEALTHIER EATING HABITS

NICHOLA LUDLAM-RAINE
BSc (hons), PG Dip, MSc

EBURY
PRESS

Ebury Press, an imprint of Ebury Publishing
20 Vauxhall Bridge Road
London SW1V 2SA

Ebury Press is part of the Penguin Random House group
of companies whose addresses can be found at
global.penguinrandomhouse.com

First published by Ebury Press in 2024

www.penguin.co.uk

A CIP catalogue record for this book is
available from the British Library

ISBN 9781529940114

Photography: Joe Woodhouse
Food Stylist: Eleanor Mulligan
Prop Stylist: Megan Thomson

Printed and bound in Great Britain by Clays Ltd, Elcograf S.p.A.

The authorised representative in the EEA is Penguin Random House
Ireland, Morrison Chambers, 32 Nassau Street, Dublin D02 YH68

Penguin Random House is committed to a sustainable future for
our business, our readers and our planet. This book is made from
Forest Stewardship Council® certified paper.

I dedicate this book to my two little children.

May you both grow up to be healthy and happy.

CONTENTS

PART THREE:
LOOKING AHEAD

A note before we begin

I have worked clinically as a dietitian for 15 years, and in all that time, I can honestly say that my eating habits and the way I viewed food hadn't really changed much at all ... until I began researching and writing this book. Before I really looked into it, I thought the conversation around ultra-processed foods (UPFs) was just healthy eating wrapped up in different paper – but I was wrong to make this assumption. Writing this book has not only allowed me to share the advice and practical tips around diet that have helped my clients and patients over the many years I've been practising, but it has also allowed me to share the new issues associated with modern-day diets and UPFs – as well as the accompanying nuances – alongside potential solutions to help.

My aim isn't for you to drastically overhaul your diet in one go, but to instead encourage you to pause and reflect on your current diet and, over the next month (and beyond!), make sustainable swaps and simple changes to improve your health not only for now, but for the future too. The information in this book applies to everyone, and although I truly believe it will help to educate and empower you, it is not a substitute for personalised advice from a healthcare professional.

PART ONE

GETTING TO KNOW UPFs

CHAPTER 1

INTRODUCTION TO UPFs

I t may be tempting to pick up this book and skip straight to the weekly plan, but having worked with thousands of people who wanted to improve their diets, I know that a diet plan alone (sadly) doesn't result in long-term change. What's needed is the backstory, and the reasons *why* change matters. During this introduction I will tell you what ultra-processed foods (UPFs) are, and why you need to pay attention to them.

Here's to improving your knowledge and your diet quality by making empowered choices, which will result in eating fewer UPFs once and for all.

WHAT ARE UPFs?

Have you been hearing more and more about UPFs (ultra-processed foods), yet are confused about what they are, as well as their importance? If the answer is yes, you're not alone! Even as a dietitian with over 15 years of clinical experience, I've had to do some serious digging, research, thinking and discussing with colleagues about what UPFs actually mean for me and my clients, and how best to translate this fairly new scientific area into practical, take-home messages regarding diet and nutrition. To put it simply though, UPFs are foods that have undergone significant processing and modification from their original state.

They are usually hyper-palatable and often contain many ingredients, including those that are not typically found in a home kitchen, such as stabilisers, emulsifiers, preservatives, colours and artificial flavourings to enhance the taste.

WHAT WILL THIS BOOK SHOW ME?

Healthy eating has become a complex web of dos and don'ts that can leave even the smartest and most well-informed people baffled. One minute we are told that a certain food should be part of our diet, then in the next breath we are told it should be banned altogether. It can be exhausting, and social media only perpetuates these confusing matters.

This is exactly why I decided to write this book – to share my knowledge and insight with anyone who is keen to know more about UPFs, or who has ever reached out to me with questions or concerns in regard to food and nutrition. This book aims to simplify the subject of UPFs, and will help you to eat fewer of them on a daily basis (in particular the less-nutritious UPFs) without feeling like you are on a diet! After all, it's not about diets, it's about a way of life.

With this book, my promise to you is this: we're going to cut through the noise and confusion in order to address UPFs more directly; we will demystify the inner workings of UPFs, and I will provide simple advice that makes sense for your everyday eating habits. Think of reading this book as like having coffee with someone who genuinely wants you to feel better, both inside and out, and is willing to share practical steps on how to achieve this.

We'll delve into what is actually in our food, discuss how to make smarter decisions and tackle questions like, 'Can I still enjoy my favourite chocolate biscuit?' Spoiler alert: yes, you can – think moderation, not deprivation! After all, life is too short to completely avoid what we love. In my dietetic practice, there is always room for 'soul foods'.

So, when you're ready, grab your favourite cuppa and your favourite unprocessed or ultra-processed snack (there's no judgement here – who doesn't love a chocolate digestive with a tea?!), and let's begin this journey of understanding and consuming fewer UPFs together.

WHAT'S THE DIFFERENCE BETWEEN UNPROCESSED, PROCESSED AND ULTRA-PROCESSED FOODS?

Let's break it down. We often hear categories of foods such as unprocessed, processed and ultra-processed, but what are the definitions of these terms? Understanding these categories in greater depth is essential for making better choices to improve our physical health, mental health and emotional wellbeing, too.

'UPFs' is a fairly recent term, first coined in 2009 when researchers at the University of São Paulo, Brazil, proposed a new classification framework, known as NOVA, for grouping foods based on the extent of their processing. The NOVA system comprises four different levels, with UPFs sitting in level 4. Although useful as a population-level tool for global organisations and governments who need to assess diets, the NOVA system wasn't designed to categorise individual foods, so I find it easiest to talk about food processing using three main groups:

Unprocessed foods*: Unprocessed foods are those that are relatively untouched, just as nature intended them. Think fruits, vegetables, potatoes, nuts, dried lentils and grains such as

---

* *Unprocessed foods may have undergone very minimal processing in order to get them from nature to your table, but in general they have not had any other ingredients added, or nutrients taken away (unlike more refined carbohydrates where some of the fibre is lost).*

wholegrain rice. These foods make it to your plate without much processing at all. Unprocessed foods are packed full of nutrients and are essential for good health.

Processed foods: So, this is when it starts getting controversial. Processed foods, as the name suggests, have been altered in some way by humans – but that does not mean they are necessarily 'bad'. For example, tinned butter beans are 'processed', as the beans have been cooked and then tinned with water, but these 'processed' beans are a wonderful source of plant-based protein as well as fibre, plus, ready-to-go beans are also super convenient, meaning you're more likely to use them than you are to use dried beans. Most milks and yoghurts have also been processed, as they're pasteurised to ensure safe consumption, but they are a great way of getting both calcium and iodine into our diets, and additionally, they help with healthy gut bacteria. Pasta is another example of a (minimally) processed food – it contains just one ingredient (wheat), but is still processed as it isn't found in nature.

Ultra-processed foods (UPFs): Now let's go one level up to ultra-processed foods (UPFs). According to the NOVA classification, UPFs have undergone significant processing and modification from their original form. UPFs also contain ingredients that aren't found in a typical home kitchen: additives including preservatives, emulsifiers, artificial colours and flavours. Typical UPFs include soft drinks and fizzy drinks, packaged snacks, reconstituted meat products, as well as pre-prepared frozen meals, which tend to contain excessive amounts of fat (saturated fat in particular), sugar, salt and calories, while falling short in essential nutrients. These foods may also be known as HFSS, which identifies foods and drinks that are high in fat (particularly saturated fat), salt and sugar. Healthier and nutritious foods may also fall under the UPF category though, including wholegrain breakfast cereals, fish fingers, supermarket sliced breads (even wholemeal) and baked beans too.

How do I know what is ultra-processed?

We'll get into how to further identify and evaluate UPFs later in this part of the book, however, as a quick cheat sheet, I have included a list of the most commonly eaten foods and drinks in the Appendix of this book (see page 259). I have divided them into four different groups: unprocessed, minimally processed, more processed yet nutritious, and more processed and less nutritious. You may find it useful to refer to this list as you work through this book:

- **GROUP 1:**
  Unprocessed
  e.g. oats, apples and potatoes

- **GROUP 2:**
  Minimally processed
  e.g. 100 per cent fruit juice, most hummus and tinned butter beans

- **GROUP 3:**
  More processed yet nutritious
  (technically UPFs)
  e.g. fish fingers, most baked beans, oat milk and some wholemeal bread

- **GROUP 4:**
  More processed and less nutritious
  (UPFs and HFSS)
  e.g. chocolate biscuits, some oven chips and crisps, and most low-calorie snack bars.

WHY DO (PROCESSED AND) ULTRA-PROCESSED FOODS (UPFs) EXIST?

The cynical answer here is that UPFs exist because a manufacturer's main aim is to make money, and processed foods containing flavourings and relatively high amounts of sugar and salt not only taste good, but they make us want to eat more too. The real answer, though, is that it doesn't just boil down to taste – ultimately, UPFs exist due to the need for preservation, logistical considerations and economics, too.

Their emergence dates back to World War II, when there was a dramatic shift in lifestyles – more women began entering the workforce, and with less time at home, families needed more convenient and quick meal options. Enter UPFs – heroes of convenience and shelf life! Let's peel back the layers in order to understand manufacturers' motivations, and to determine how and why UPFs exist at all.

Preserve food for longer: the miracle of shelf-life preservation

In large part, UPFs exist for one main reason: preservation. Before refrigeration and modern food processing methods were available, preserving food was essential. People needed a means of keeping it safe for longer. This led to canning, drying, salting and, later on, more complex methods like adding preservatives and emulsifiers – techniques that not only extend shelf life but help preserve texture and nutritional value too; think tinned vegetables or dried fruits – convenient options that let us enjoy off-season produce all year round.

Transportation: on a global scale

Have you ever gone to the supermarket and been surprised when a certain food is not there? We expect an abundance of foods to be presented to us every day of the year, and in order to provide access to this wide range of diverse foods, UPFs have been specially engineered so that food items can withstand the long journey from farms to factories (across the world), to supermarkets and then onto our plates. While this has revolutionised our eating habits, it has also led to the widespread popularity of heavily processed products.

Economic considerations: the cost factor

UPFs are cheaper to produce and are therefore more accessible to people and families with small budgets.* Plus their longer shelf life means less food waste, which is also necessary for some families.

Convenience: time-saving and eating on the move

Don't overlook the convenience factor. Time is precious in our hectic world, especially since World War II, with most adults working at least a nine to five (and often more). Cooking from scratch is hard when time is scarce, and UPFs can offer quick and convenient meal solutions that assist busy lifestyles. Ready meals, instant noodles, frozen chips and microwave pizzas are popular as they are convenient and quick to prepare, and other UPFs such as packaged sandwiches, bottled fizzy drinks

---

It must be acknowledged that there is often a financial cost and privilege when it comes to avoiding or reducing UPFs, as cooking more from scratch and preparing foods takes knowledge as well as time and cooking equipment. This book aims to provide you with the knowledge to make informed decisions and choices about food within your own personal means.

and snack bars are ideal for eating and drinking on the go – a common trait of modern-day life.

The rise in free-from and veganism: dietary requirements

My son has several food allergies, including dairy, eggs and soya, so I can safely say that without 'free-from' foods (most of which are classified as UPFs) and plant-based alternatives, I would struggle to feed him a balanced diet containing all the nutrients he needs. He has drunk oat milk (fortified with calcium) since he was a toddler, eats frozen fish fingers on an almost weekly basis for the omega-3 and iodine (I get the ones branded as high in omega-3) and his bread has to be carefully selected when we're at the supermarket to make sure it doesn't contain soya flour (the majority do) – so these restrictions cut our choices down dramatically. However, he has his oat milk on a high-fibre cereal (wheat biscuits most of the time, with banana), and has peas with his fish fingers and baked beans (sigh, yet another UPF, we just cannot escape them!), meaning that overall, he does eat a nutritious and balanced diet.

As you can see, even dietitians (and children of!) do not eat a completely UPF-free diet, as the right UPFs *can* add nutritional value. 'Good' and 'bad' binary thinking when it comes to unprocessed foods versus UPFs, isn't helpful and can cause unnecessary anxiety, as we shall explore later.

UPFs ARE A DOUBLE-EDGED SWORD

It is essential to recognise that while UPFs provide some long-term advantages, such as longer shelf life and affordability, they may contain a greater amount of added sugars, unhealthy fats and sodium (salt) than less-processed foods, and may also fall short in essential vitamins, which could contribute to health issues if too many UPFs are consumed over time (quantity and context matters here). This is in addition to UPFs often having additional flavourings, colours, emulsifiers, stabilisers and preservatives added to them, too.

There is evidence to suggest that people also eat *more* when consuming a diet that is high in ultra-processed foods, which can lead to weight gain and poorer health outcomes. Researchers aren't entirely sure why this happens, as it may not just be down to sheer palatability, but rather due to the easy-to-eat nature of the foods, which could lead to delayed satiety signalling.

What are emulsifiers? Are they all bad?

Emulsifiers are additives that help to stabilise processed foods, meaning they stop ingredients that wouldn't usually mix, such as oil and water, from separating. They help to provide texture and increase shelf life too. There are questions regarding the impact of consuming large amounts of certain emulsifiers on the gut microbiome, however the effects are likely individual and more research is needed. Some small studies on animals (rodents) have found gut bacteria to be impacted by very large amounts of specific emulsifiers, which caused intestinal inflammation. But evidence is limited to only a few emulsifiers, and the gastrointestinal effects in humans from long-term consumption of large amounts of common emulsifiers are currently largely unknown.

What I would like you to remember, though, is that emulsifiers are generally present in foods in very small amounts – for example, soya lecithin, an emulsifier that is found in dark chocolate. What matters most when it comes to health (including our gut health) is our diet as a whole,

---

i.e. what you are mainly eating. Cutting down on the number of UPFs in your diet will mean that you will naturally be eating fewer emulsifiers, so please don't worry about the effects of consuming small amounts. I have included more information about specific emulsifiers in the Appendix of this book (see page 263).

As we explore UPFs further, let's keep in mind that they exist for many valid reasons, and it is up to us to navigate the terrain wisely if we wish to enjoy their benefits and not miss out on social occasions (not everyone has the time or skills to make a homemade birthday cake, for example!), while making decisions that support our health. There is a complex relationship between naturalness, food processing and healthiness, particularly when it comes to UPFs, which is an extremely diverse category. To say that *all* UPFs are unnatural and not nutritious is not entirely true, and hopefully this book will help you to realise that we can't be so binary when it comes to labelling food that has been processed in some way.

THE NUTRITIONAL SPECTRUM OF UPFs

Herein lies the challenge, for not all UPFs are created equal when it comes to their nutritional content. Some pre-packaged, unflavoured or flavoured porridge (the pots that you add boiling water to), for example, might technically count as UPFs, but they can still form part of a nutritious (and convenient) diet. Yet on the other hand, a bag of crisps also counts as a UPF, but has lower nutritional values, with more salt and a less than ideal macronutrient composition. Crisps can still feature in a healthy balanced diet, of course, but the key is to manage portion size and frequency of consumption, as we will discuss. Making informed choices requires understanding this spectrum and being aware of all of the options available to us at any given time.

As we move forward, keep in mind that in order to foster both health and happiness we need to understand what we are eating, we need to know how to make informed (healthy) choices and, most importantly, we need to enjoy the variety of food available to us (ultra-processed or not!).

Let's look, then, at a high-UPF day versus a low-UPF day, to see how easy it is to consume a lot of convenience foods, and how you can begin making tweaks to live a more unprocessed life.

High-UPF day's diet

Breakfast	A bowl of chocolate- or honey-coated cereal with milk, served alongside a shop-bought orange juice drink (with added sugar and sweetener) and an instant latte sachet containing multiple ingredients not usually found in a home kitchen.
Morning snack	A packaged snack bar and a can of full-sugar fizzy drink.
Lunch	A microwavable ready meal (such as a pepperoni pizza or a cheeseburger) that can be quickly heated and eaten within minutes.
Afternoon snack	A packet of crisps, a chocolate bar and a diet cola to satisfy hunger pangs.
Evening meal	Takeaway fried chicken with chips, followed by a shop-bought chocolate pudding.
Dessert/ evening snack	A supermarket cookie, more crisps and an instant hot chocolate while watching TV.

Low-UPF day's diet

Breakfast	A bowl of overnight oats made with milk and plain yoghurt, topped with fresh or frozen berries and crushed mixed nuts, along with a small glass (150ml) of freshly squeezed or 100 per cent pure orange juice.
Morning snack	Seasonal fruit (fresh or dried) with almonds or walnuts.
Lunch	A homemade salad made up of various fresh vegetables, grilled chicken breast, couscous and an olive oil and vinegar dressing.
Afternoon snack	A homemade oat-based snack bar.
Evening meal	Baked salmon, accompanied by steamed broccoli and homemade sweet potato wedges.
Dessert/ evening snack	Greek yoghurt topped with a drizzle of honey, strawberries and homemade granola with raisins. Herbal tea.

In the high-UPF day's diet, we observe convenience and speed – with minimal thought and no preparation required, meals can be ready quickly, yet they are often high in additives, sugars, unhealthy fats and sodium (salt), while also lacking essential nutrients. By contrast, in the low-UPF day's diet, we observe whole, minimally processed foods which provide more nutrition and fibre, but which also require more time and effort to prepare – this may not be achievable or sustainable for everyone all of the time.

This comparison isn't about labelling one day as 'bad' and one day as 'good', rather it aims to heighten the awareness of just how many options we are faced with every single day when it comes to our food – choices that will ultimately affect our health and wellbeing.

Pause to reflect. How did you feel reading the two diets shown? Can you relate to either? Are there variations in your own eating habits, with some days leaning towards a higher-UPF diet, and others leaning towards a lower-UPF diet? What factors influence your food choices?

As we navigate the vast realm of ultra-processed foods, it's essential to recognise that not all UPFs are the same. There is a spectrum of choice, from more nutritious to less nutritious. Let's look at a day where processed foods and UPFs *are* consumed, but more-nutritious UPF choices are made over some less-nutritious UPF options.

High-UPF (more nutritious) day's diet

Breakfast	Fortified breakfast cereal* high in fibre, calcium and other essential vitamins and minerals including iron, with semi-skimmed milk and a sliced banana (fruit is not a UPF, and milk isn't considered a UPF either, even though it is processed during pasteurisation).
Morning snack	A protein bar – high in protein and low in sugar.
Lunch	A pre-packaged (long-life) tuna salad containing lentils, carrots, chickpeas, red peppers and a honey and ginger dressing. Water to drink.
Afternoon snack	Baked crisps and fruit.
Evening meal	Frozen breaded chicken (grilled) in a wholemeal wrap* with fresh salad (salad is not a UPF).
Dessert/ evening snack	Low-sugar fruit yoghurt and an oat-based snack bar.*

---

* *These foods can be UPFs or non-UPFs depending on their ingredients.*

This day shows more of a balance when it comes to both convenience *and* health. Fortified UPFs (ones that are higher in fibre, protein and essential nutrients, while being lower in sugar and unhealthy fats) are prioritised, such as high-fibre cereal and wholemeal wraps.

UPFs, then, can be convenient and tasty options, and they don't (all) need to be viewed as negative, as it's the portion size and frequency with which we eat all foods that matters most. My aim is not to demonise UPFs (far from it), but rather to help you to make better choices that will lead you to habitual healthier eating in the long term. Together, we can better navigate the complex world of processed and ultra-processed food, in order to meet our health goals and needs effectively.

SO UPFs AREN'T BAD FOR US?

We've just explored how UPFs can have a (very convenient) place in our busy daily lives. But let's get into this discussion, exploring the concerns and recommendations around UPFs.

As mentioned previously, a higher intake of UPFs has been linked with various health problems, including weight gain, which can be a risk factor for conditions such as type 2 diabetes and cardiovascular disease. This may be because many UPFs contain more calories (they are often energy dense), sugars, salt and unhealthy fats and lack essential nutrients such as fibre. In addition, lots of UPFs tend not to be very filling, and research shows that certain additives and flavour combinations can lead to addictive eating behaviours (once you pop ...). In addition to promoting overconsumption, UPFs can also end up displacing more nutritional unprocessed and minimally processed foods from our diets. It doesn't stop there, either – some UPFs have additional detrimental health impacts such as tooth decay (fizzy drinks and high-sugar snacks are the culprits here) and changes in gut health, as we have previously discussed.

There are, of course, many factors that influence our health (our genetics, our access to healthcare and our social class, to name just a few!), and the research on the impact of UPFs so far does not prove cause and effect. However, the body of evidence linking a high intake of UPFs with health problems is growing, and with 50 per cent of the average diet (and up to 80 per cent in some people) now being made up of UPFs, health professionals are paying attention and are turning to the government to try to change this. Some people are even beginning to ask questions about the impacts of high-UPF diets and common mental health disorders. Despite this, the link between high-UPF diets and mental health is still far from clear, and will be difficult to unpick. This is due to the complex genetic, psychological and social factors that contribute to the development of mental health problems, not to mention the impact that struggling with mental health in and of itself might have on diet quality.

The Scientific Advisory Committee on Nutrition (SACN) in the UK has voiced concern over UPF consumption, noting how higher-UPF diets have been linked with poorer health outcomes (in particular for those who eat large amounts of them). But SACN also acknowledges that the current understanding of UPFs is limited. For instance, although the NOVA classification system (which categorises foods into four different processing levels) is helpful, it still leaves room for data error, and more research is needed in order to better comprehend the health impacts, as well as the place of UPFs within modern-day diets.

The foods that large health agencies such as the World Health Organization all agree we should be eating less of include red and processed meats, the latter of which mostly falls into the category of UPFs. We will be discussing this topic in more depth later, but while having fresh, lean red meat two to three times a week may be within the realms of a healthy and balanced diet (lean red meat is a good source of easy-to-absorb iron), processed red meats such as ham, bacon, gammon and sausages should be eaten infrequently due to high intakes being linked with bowel cancer.

So, as you're probably realising by now, although it may be tempting to view all UPFs as 'bad', their true impact is more complex, and what matters most is portion size and the frequency with which you consume them, in addition to the type of foods you are consuming most of the time. If you eat a mainly whole-food, unprocessed diet, the odd UPF isn't going to be an issue, especially if it's on the more-nutritious end of the spectrum.

So what can we take away from all this? We can comfortably conclude that balance and informed choices are the cornerstones of good health. UPFs are a part of modern life, and we can make decisions that will help us to maintain a healthy lifestyle – no matter how busy we may become.

WHAT ABOUT SUGAR?

Table sugar (also known as sucrose) isn't classed as a UPF on its own, however it is found in many, if not the majority of UPFs on the market. Discussing sugar as a whole topic, however, requires nuanced consideration. While excessive sugar intake can be harmful to teeth and is linked to obesity, type 2 diabetes and other health conditions, its form and quantity matters. Natural sugars, found, for example, in fruits and milk, differ significantly from the added sugars found in UPFs, where moderation is key.

Let me explain a little further. Sugar is a type of carbohydrate, which include starches and sugars. Carbohydrates, specifically sugar (glucose), are our brains' primary fuel source, but our muscles use a mixture of both fats and carbohydrates for fuel – the ratio of which varies depending on demands (exercise intensity). When it comes to health, the type and portion size of the carbohydrates we consume matters, with fruits and milk (natural sugars), vegetables and wholegrain carbohydrates (starches) providing more nutrients than table sugar.

The government recommends that we limit our total sugar intake to no more than 90g a day, and our free-sugar intake to no more than 30g a day. Free-sugar includes table sugar (sucrose), sugars added by manufacturers to foods, as well as the sugar found naturally in fruit juice and honey. The natural sugars in whole fruits are not classed as free-sugars, as they are unprocessed and because fruit also contains fibre.

One of the issues when it comes to reading food labels is that manufacturers do not differentiate between the sugars that are naturally occurring and the free-sugars in a product (the latter of which are easier to overconsume and may be more harmful to health). This is why it is often more useful to look at the ingredients list instead. You will naturally start to do this more as you try to work out how many UPFs (and more importantly, what type!) are making their way into your diet. If sugar* or a syrup is near the start of the ingredients list, it means that there is a lot of added sugar within the product (relatively speaking), which implies that it could be a UPF and should therefore be consumed in moderation, and certainly less often than a more nutritious or whole-food equivalent.

---

* *Sugar on the ingredients list can come in many different guises, including agave nectar, cane sugar, coconut sugar, maltose and palm sugar – don't be fooled by a fancy name, sugar is sugar.*

Did you know that when you look at a label on a flavoured yoghurt, the sugar listed in grams in the nutritional information includes the natural sugar from the milk used to make the yoghurt (lactose), any fruit that is included (fructose) and any table sugar (sucrose) that has been added, too? If you want to find out the actual amount of *added* sugar in a pre-flavoured yoghurt, compare a plain yoghurt's sugar per 100g to that of a UPF yoghurt's, and you will have your answer.

Are sweeteners any better?

Artificial sweeteners are commonplace amongst UPFs and continue to spark controversy as sugar substitutes. Artificial sweeteners such as aspartame and sucralose, or more natural sweeteners such as stevia, may offer sweetness without calories, but their potential impact on gut health and weight management are the subjects of ongoing study and debate, with conflicting findings depending on which studies you look at. The impact of artificial sweeteners on humans varies greatly depending on the individual. More research is needed in this area and is currently being undertaken.

The European Food Safety Authority (EFSA) plays a key role in checking the safety of the artificial sweeteners used within Europe. All sweeteners undergo strict and rigorous safety tests and checks, and to further ensure their safety, the Acceptable Daily Intake (ADI) levels are set at 100 times lower than the amount it would actually be safe to consume. Take aspartame, for example. In order to exceed the ADI for this sweetener, a person who weighs around 70kg would have to drink 14 cans of diet fizzy drink a day, which is way more than what most people consume. Times this by 100, and the actual figure is 140 cans.

Your teeth would likely rot due to the acidity of the drink before its sweeteners harmed your health.

In my opinion, sweeteners offer the pleasure of sweetness without the additional calories associated with sugar, making them an invaluable asset to weight management and controlling blood sugar levels, particularly among those living with diabetes. In addition, their dental-health benefits cannot be discounted, since, unlike sugar, they don't contribute to tooth decay, as oral bacteria cannot ferment them into plaque.

As a dietitian, I would always recommend that my patients choose a diet drink over the full-sugar version, however as both are very obvious (non-nutritious) UPFs, it would be much healthier to drink water instead. This isn't always desirable though, which is why we have to look at the bigger picture and ask ourselves how often these drinks are creeping into our diet – once a week at the pub on a Friday night is nothing, for example, in comparison to someone who fuels their entire day with it, most days of the week.

Our aim should always be to cut down on our fizzy drink consumption, and we will discuss this more later, but for now, if you don't experience any unwanted side effects from sweetened fizzy drinks, or from sweeteners in general, then they can safely be consumed in moderation.

WHAT ABOUT FAT?

Fats were once unfairly demonised, with many manufacturers, as well as weight loss companies, jumping on the bandwagon by producing low-fat and fat-free UPFs. Some fats, however, are essential to health – as the body cannot make them – and fat helps the body to absorb the fat-soluble vitamins A, D, E and K.

Dietary guidelines recommend that we moderate our fat intake, and replace saturated fats with unsaturated fats. Most foods contain a mix of both saturated and unsaturated fats, with the latter being preferred for health. Foods rich in unsaturated fats include plant sources such as olive oil, rapeseed oil, avocados, nuts and seeds, as well as oily fish such as salmon and mackerel – we should aim for at least one portion of oily fish a week for the unsaturated omega-3 fatty acids that they provide. Pure fats are relatively energy dense however (providing nine calories per gram, in comparison to carbohydrates and protein, which provide around four calories per gram), meaning they should be consumed in moderation. I often advise my patients to use around half a tablespoon of oil (olive oil or rapeseed oil) per portion in cooking.

So, should you stop buying low-fat or fat-free foods? The answer is that it entirely depends on what it is and what has been added to compensate. Plain yoghurt, for example, won't have any sugar added, but a fruit-flavoured yoghurt may have. The main message to take away is to not automatically assume that foods labelled as 'low-fat' or 'fat-free' are healthy, as marshmallows, for example, are often labelled as being fat-free (but are loaded with added sugar!).

HOW TO FIND BALANCE WITH UPFs: THE 80/20 RULE

I have been shouting about this 'rule' or guideline for more than a decade, as it offers the perfect balance between eating to nourish ourselves and not missing out on the fun foods and drinks that we enjoy.

So, what does this 'rule' mean? It means that around 80 per cent of our dietary intake should consist of whole and minimally processed foods, while leaving 20 per cent for convenience, fun and enjoyment from UPFs, if desired. This approach doesn't advocate limiting or restricting our food consumption by any means; it instead suggests finding a more sustainable balance in our eating habits, both for health, and for socialising too.

Another way of looking at this 'rule' is to follow healthy eating guidelines around 80 per cent of the time (think more plant-based foods here!), and the other 20 per cent to do whatever you fancy. A little of what you like does you good, after all!

Do all UPFs count towards the 20 per cent?

One of the fascinating aspects of UPFs is their wide-ranging nutritional profiles. Take, for instance, baked beans and chocolate biscuits – two UPFs but with vastly different nutritional profiles. Baked beans contain mainly beans and tomatoes, providing protein, fibre and vitamins too, while chocolate biscuits often feature high amounts of sugar and saturated fat with minimal nutritional benefit. I would personally therefore include baked beans in my 80 per cent and chocolate biscuits in my 20 per cent. Use the Appendix in the back of this book (see page 259) to learn about the more-nutritious and less-nutritious UPF options.

SHOULD I EAT VEGAN?

As we work to reduce our consumption of UPFs, a plant-based and/or vegan diet may seem like an attractive way of eating more healthily (due to an overall higher fibre and nutrient content) and responsibly (due to a smaller carbon footprint). In general, a vegan diet emphasises the benefits of plant-derived foods such as fruits, vegetables, grains, nuts, seeds and legumes, and excludes all animal products, but there are still many ultra-processed vegan options out there. Let's look at what considerations need to be taken when adopting a plant-based and/or a vegan diet.

The pros of plant-based and vegan diets

Plant-based and vegan diets offer significant health benefits when planned carefully – they can be lifestyle choices with profoundly positive outcomes. Packed with nutrients and fibre, and often lower in calories and unhealthy fats when compared to their traditional counterparts, plant-based and vegan diets have the power to promote heart health and weight management and to reduce the risk of some chronic diseases if executed well. However, it is imperative to do your homework when planning any such diet, particularly regarding UPFs.

The cons of plant-based and vegan diets: watch out for vegan junk food!

Those following a vegan diet may make the mistaken assumption that all vegan products are nutritious (and non-UPF). Unfortunately, the truth is that many vegan products are highly processed; vegan cookies and confectionery, some meat substitutes* and pre-packaged meals made without animal products might still contain high levels of unhealthy fats, sugars and salt and additives – making them UPFs. One of the reasons for this is that foods such as eggs (eggs are a non-UPF) are often used as a binder, and when you start to remove such foods, other additives, such as emulsifiers, have to be introduced so the product doesn't fall apart (literally!).

Not all meat substitutes need to be avoided, it's just that you may have to be more mindful regarding the total amount of salt you are having from other pre-prepared foods (aim to keep to less than 6g of salt a day).

Supplementation (or fortification) is also necessary on a vegan diet to avoid nutritional deficiencies.* Pay attention to the following if you are consuming a strictly vegan diet:

- **Protein:** opt for foods such as wholegrains, beans, lentils, chickpeas, tofu and quinoa at every meal.

- **Vitamin B12:** as B12 is found in animal products, look for vitamin B12 on the ingredients list to make sure your breakfast cereal has been fortified with B12, and consider buying nutritional yeast fortified with B12 to sprinkle on pastas, risottos and soups. A supplement may also be needed.

- **Iron:** while plant-based iron (non-haem iron) may be less easily absorbed by your body, consuming vitamin C-rich foods at the same time as consuming iron-rich foods can increase absorption rates. Simply squeeze a bit of lemon or lime onto foods, or add tomatoes to a bean- or lentil-based dish.

- **Calcium and vitamin D:** for bone health purposes, fortified plant milks provide important sources of these essential vitamins, in addition to the mineral iodine. Check on the back of the package that these nutrients have been added (it should be listed under the ingredients list). In addition, make sure any tofu that you buy contains calcium on the ingredients list too. An additional vitamin D supplement may also be required, particularly in the winter months (everyone living in the UK should consider taking a 10mcg vitamin D supplement from late September to the end of March).

- **Omega-3 fatty acids:** flaxseeds (also known as linseeds), chia seeds and walnuts are plant-based sources of omega-3

---

* *For more information on the nutrients required to support a healthy vegan diet, check out the Vegan Society website and resources.*

and can be added to breakfasts or into smoothies. An algae-based supplement may also be of benefit.

One of the best ways to 'unprocess' your life is to cook the majority of your own meals, whether you're vegan or not. Doing so gives you complete control over the ingredients and methods you use, and helps you to discover the joy of homemade meals!

SHOULD I BE EATING 30 PLANTS A WEEK?

If you're keen to eat healthily, then you may have heard about the benefits of eating at least 30 different plant-based foods a week. These foods are naturally non-UPF and include fruits, vegetables, wholegrains, legumes, nuts and seeds, and spices too. Variety is key to a healthy diet and ultimately, the more plants you can eat, the better, but research shows that eating at least 30 different plants a week helps to increase the diversity and, in turn, the health of the gut microbiome. A healthier gut can mean improved health, with possible benefits being seen on both the immune system and mood too.

Although 30 sounds like a large number, it can easily be achieved within the context of a balanced diet, as different colours of the same fruit and vegetable count as different plants (for example, a red pepper and a yellow pepper count as two plants), and adding a handful of mixed seeds including pumpkin, sesame and sunflower to your porridge would be an easy additional three plants. Spices also count as a quarter of a plant per serving, which means adding cinnamon and ginger to your next bowl of porridge would be an extra half a plant!

Diets rich in plants give us an array of beneficial compounds, including antioxidants and fibre, which improves digestion and reduces the risk of some diseases. We should aim to eat at least 30g of fibre a day, however the majority of us are not reaching anywhere near this figure.

Focusing on eating more plants should mean that there is naturally less room for UPFs,* which is a win-win when it comes to health.

Do I have to go vegan for my health (and the planet)?

No, you don't! But eating a more plant-based or plant-focused diet is beneficial for the planet and you too – make vegetables the stars of your plate! Be wary of 'health halos' though – this is a tactic used by the food industry to draw your attention to one aspect of a food, making you believe it is 'healthy' in order to influence your purchasing habits, when in reality, the claims may not reflect the whole product. Just because a product is plant-based or vegan doesn't automatically make it non-UPF, so you'll need to read the ingredients list to know for sure.

WHEN YOU'RE FEEDING A FAMILY

Carers and parents play a crucial role in looking after children's health and their dietary habits. Part of this may involve critically assessing popular products, such as energy drinks, which older children may ask for. As adults, it is important to lead by example and to consume more unprocessed, whole foods. Family

---

* *Recent analysis shows that UPFs high in wholegrains and fibre (including breakfast cereals and breads), which improve digestion, may not significantly contribute to the negative associations observed between a high UPF intake and increased risk factors for some diseases.*

mealtimes are a great time to set good examples, with the key being to educate children from a young age, and to involve them in cooking as much as possible. UPFs (particularly the less-nutritious kind) should not be touted as 'bad' however, but rather be described as foods that are not eaten as often as non-UPF foods, which in general provide much more in the way of 'goodness' for our bodies.

The topic of UPFs can be a source of anxiety for many parents, especially as children go through fussy phases and may also have food allergies. Keep in mind that there is no single right way to eat, and it's what children and teenagers are eating the majority of the time that matters most. Encourage your kids to eat their five a day (eat a rainbow!), and use the information in this book to tackle one family meal at a time. Ask your doctor for a referral to a dietitian, or talk to a registered nutritionist who specialises in children if you have any specific concerns.

I spoke to a well-known, trustworthy baby and toddler food brand whose products I personally have bought for years, and they had the following to say about UPFs, which is in line with the philosophy of this book:

> We are committed to making great quality food for children, using organically sourced ingredients, which are nutritious and offer breadth of choice and variety to parents. All our food is specifically created for babies and toddlers and goes through rigorous checks to ensure it meets strict safety and nutritional standards.
>
> Recent media coverage and reports on ultra-processed foods come from a definition set by the NOVA food classification system. However, having done our own research and in-depth analysis of the classification, we believe it can be misleading for consumers. This is because it does not follow any reasonable criteria from a nutritional

point of view. Not all ultra-processed foods are unhealthy; they can also include foods that are part of a healthy diet such as wholemeal sliced bread, lower-sugar yoghurts, wholegrain breakfast cereals or baked beans. It's important not to demonise foods based solely on processing.

We support eating well in the early years in line with public health recommendations and we strive to create foods that have positive nutritional value for little ones. All our foods clearly list all ingredients and their nutritional values so customers can make clear and informed decisions.

Recent studies have shown the negative consequences of consuming energy drinks, including anxiety, stress and physical-health concerns. As a result, these products should not be given to children or teenagers. No-added-sugar squash mixed with sparkling water can be a healthier alternative to fizzy drinks.

KEY TAKEAWAYS FROM THIS INTRODUCTION

- UPFs exist for many reasons, including preservation and convenience.

- UPFs are not all bad, and it is important to look at the overall nutritional quality and the ingredients list of a product in order to make informed decisions about how often the food should be eaten.

- Eating healthily is not about never touching a doughnut again, but enjoying UPFs in moderation.

- It is possible to follow a UPF-free diet, but how far you take this is up to you. I personally advocate the 80/20 rule, and throughout this book will be providing options for whatever life may throw at you.

- It is not necessary to follow a vegan diet for health, but eating more plants is good for health and good for the planet, too.

- If you're a parent, focus on setting a good example at mealtimes by modelling a healthy relationship with food. You can achieve this by avoiding moralising about foods (e.g. by not labelling foods 'good' and 'bad') and by eating a variety of whole foods at mealtimes.

CHAPTER 2

HOW TO USE THIS BOOK

Now that we've discussed the 'whats', 'whys' and nuances of UPFs, we're ready to get into the nuts and bolts of how to start consuming fewer of them.

Food choices have the ability to move you either closer to or further away from your health goals, and this book is going to teach you how to make informed choices at every eating opportunity. As a part of our plan to reduce our consumption of UPFs, it is important to look at both the quantity and the quality of those we currently eat, as well as where easy swaps to non-UPFs (i.e. non- and minimally processed foods) can be made. The aim should be to recognise which UPFs are creeping into our diets, as well as which are more nutrient dense than others. Every food decision counts as we strive to reduce our overall intake of UPFs, but at the same time, it's important not to miss out on life's little pleasures. The aim of this book is to allow you to enjoy all foods, especially when it comes to eating socially.

So let your health transformation begin. Don't try to read this book cover to cover all in one go; instead, digest the practical tips slowly and implement them one by one. We will tackle each mealtime together in order to make small changes that, when done consistently over time (by habit!), will lead to big results. We will start with tackling snacks and drinks, before moving on to breakfast, lunch and finally the evening meal (I won't start the 'dinner' versus 'tea' debate now, but I am Northern born and bred!). Why start with snacks and drinks? Snacks and drinks are, in my opinion, one of the easiest places to start, and because we consume them frequently, changes in them can lead to big results. The key is to help you feel successful in your endeavours, as success breeds confidence, which in turn gives you the motivation to continue making changes.

Remember that this plan is meant to be flexible; so if lunch is your top concern, feel free to start there first. However, I highly suggest reading through all of this book at some point – as you never know when you might uncover additional nuggets of knowledge! Make sure to read the following chapter (Chapter 3) to prepare yourself for a successful month ahead, and the Introduction (Chapter 1) is imperative for helping you to understand the 'whats' and 'whys' of UPFs that are needed in order to make this plan stick, so do go back and read that if you haven't already.

This book will take you through one mealtime per week, and within each mealtime we will cover:

- **UPF examples:** comparing high- and low-nutritional UPFs, as well as non-UPF alternatives.

- **Common issues relating to UPFs at that mealtime:** with strategies and meal ideas to help reduce your UPF intake.

- **Organisational tips:** how you can set up your kitchen or eating space so you can more easily make healthy decisions.

- **A five-step checklist:** helping you set goals for the week, stay on track and see how far you have come.

- **Healthy recipes:** so you can enjoy delicious, yet straight-forward dishes that align with each week's focus.

- **A weekly plan for the mealtime in question, with healthy suggestions:** feel free to customise these as you wish, or to include your own healthy recipes as desired. Don't introduce lots of 'new' recipes in one go, as this will likely feel overwhelming. Start with one or two 'new' meals per week maximum, and go from there.

HOW TO USE THIS PLAN IF
YOU'RE A SHIFT WORKER

Managing mealtimes can be trickier if you work shifts, but it is still possible to instil some structure and regularity, in addition to consuming fewer UPFs. Have a look at the example plans that follow to see how eating may vary from a day shift to a night shift. Timings of meals and snacks can of course be altered to suit your specific needs.

Day shift example

6am	Get up and have a glass of water
7am	Breakfast
10am	Morning snack
12pm	Lunch
3pm	Afternoon snack
6pm	Evening meal
7 or 8pm	Optional dessert, evening snack or drink

Night shift example

5pm	Get up and have a glass of water
6pm	Evening meal or 'breakfast'
9pm	First snack
11pm	'Lunch'
2am	Second snack
5am	Breakfast or 'evening meal'
6 or 7am	Optional dessert, snack or drink

If your job or lifestyle requires you to keep unconventional hours, have a think about meal timings before you embark on this plan. What eating times work best for you and your lifestyle?

CHAPTER 3

LET'S GET READY – THE PRE-PLAN PLAN

Welcome to the first step of your journey to reduce your overall UPF intake (in particular the less nutritious options) – preparation. As the saying goes, 'Failing to prepare is preparing to fail', and this is never truer than when it comes to changing eating habits. But do not worry, this four-week plan (with an optional week five), will guide you through step by step.

We need to start with a little psychology, because humans are complex creatures, and as you'll most likely know, it's not as simple as being told to change something and then changing it. Understanding *why* we are eating is just as important as understanding *what* we are eating.

WHY DO WE EAT UPFs, EVEN WHEN THEY'RE NOT GOOD FOR US?

We eat food, including UPFs, for many reasons. In my clinic and with clients, I usually divide the reason *why* we eat into three different types of hunger: head, heart and stomach hunger. We'll be using these terms when we begin our food diary later in this chapter.

Head hunger

Food marketing is clever, and our 'food environment' can pull us into thinking about and wanting particular foods. Head hunger is the random food cravings you may get, that are often triggered by 'eye hunger' or visual cues – like when you see fresh bread being made in a bakery, or when you see enticing pictures of food while scrolling social media. Head hunger can also be triggered by hearing foods being opened, for example, when a friend opens up a crisp packet and dives in for the first crunchy bite, and smelling foods too (this is why some supermarkets have been known to pump bakery smells into the air towards unsuspecting shoppers!).

This type of hunger tends to arise suddenly and demands to be satisfied almost instantly, although you may not feel completely satiated after. You may also find that you develop a craving for a *specific* food. Of course, it's great to try new foods, variety is the spice of life after all, however, it can be costly for our wallets as well as our health, depending on the type of food being craved!

Heart hunger

Heart hunger is triggered or caused by emotions (both negative and positive). For example, eating for celebration or commiseration. Emotional eating can distract us (temporarily) from uncomfortable feelings, and can provide an instant feeling of comfort. Food can be a tool to soothe emotions (it may be known as a 'pacifier of emotions'). Although using food as a reward or pick-me-up from time to time isn't necessarily a bad thing, it can be if it becomes the only or primary coping mechanism.

If emotional eating happens on a regular basis, it can be easy to fall into an unhealthy cycle where the real feelings or issues are not being addressed. Emotional eating can also lead to further emotions, for example if a packet of biscuits is eaten out of boredom, anger or upset, it could lead to feelings of frustration or even guilt afterwards.*

Stomach hunger

With stomach hunger, we may experience the more physical feelings of hunger that come from the body, which can include a rumbling tummy, a feeling of being 'hangry', impatient or even fatigued/lightheaded. In comparison to 'head hunger', stomach hunger comes on gradually and builds until we eat again and, in comparison to 'heart hunger', eating to satisfy stomach hunger is not a way of seeking emotional solace.

We need food for both energy and nutrients, so it's important to satisfy this hunger and not put it off until it's 'too late'. If we're ravenous when it comes to eating again, it can be easy to eat too quickly, potentially causing us to overeat until we're at the other end of the hunger scale, feeling uncomfortably or painfully full. It's useful to pay attention to how your stomach hunger responds to different foods on the processing scale – as we will discuss later – in addition to staying hydrated throughout the day, too.

> Pause for reflection. Have a think about the reasons why you eat certain foods. What did you eat yesterday? Can you notice any triggers to your eating habits? Is it to do with your food environment, social media, emotions, or an erratic eating pattern perhaps, which includes not eating enough and then becoming ravenous?

---

* *If you are experiencing difficulties with cycles of emotional eating, please speak to your GP as well as the eating disorder charity BEAT.*

HOW TO MANAGE THE
DIFFERENT TYPES OF HUNGER

Let's now take a look at how we can begin to manage head, heart and stomach hunger.

Head hunger: review your environment

One of the keys to managing cravings for (less nutritious) UPFs is to modify your environment. Start by unfollowing social media pages that can trigger your cravings and need for food (if relevant) and consider your day-to-day triggers – do you need to walk a different way home from work, for example, to avoid the smell of sausage rolls from the local bakery, or should you perhaps do the weekly shop online or with a shopping list, in order to avoid the tempting brightly coloured packets? There are more practical steps you can take in order to encourage healthier cravings or to make more mindful choices – for example, by placing more fruit and vegetables in your eyesight (think a bowl of fruit and crudités in the fridge) to make the healthy choice the easy choice! More on this later though.

Let's take action. It may be helpful to break down your head hunger and cravings for UPFs into a five-step process:

1   **Recognise your triggers for UPFs:** is it being in a particular environment? At a specific time, for example at the start of your favourite TV show? When you're scrolling through social media food pages? Make a note of when and where your cravings for UPFs seem to occur.

2   **Make a plan:** once you've identified your triggers, make an alternative plan to break the habit with a positive (not negative!) intention. For example, 'At 3pm I will have a balanced snack' (e.g. a plain yoghurt with fruit, nuts

and a little honey) instead of, 'I'm not going to have biscuits this afternoon'.

3 **Identify what you really need:** changing your scenery and environment can help to squash unhelpful food cravings. Whether it's going for a walk, having a bubble bath or doing crafts – focusing your mind elsewhere can be useful!

4 **Remove visual triggers:** if you live with others and would like to reduce your consumption of certain foods (i.e. to cut down on less nutritious UPFs), try placing these out of sight – for example, in opaque containers towards the back of cupboards/fridges, or moving the biscuit tin so it is not next to the kettle. Place foods that you *would* like to be eating at the front of your cupboards/fridge and make them easily accessible around your kitchen.

5 **Learn to eat mindfully:** mindful eating is a practice that helps you to develop an awareness of your experiences, physical and emotional cues, and feelings about food. When we savour food that we consider to be a treat, we create long-lasting pleasurable experiences. By eating the majority of your meals, snacks and 'treats' mindfully, you will increase the pleasurable experience for all foods (and not just UPFs that are higher in sugar/fat), and this will help with heart hunger too.

Heart hunger: practise mindfulness

Mindfulness can be helpful when it comes to 'eating our emotions'. Take time, before and during eating, to appreciate the taste and texture of the food – and this applies to all foods, whether they are ultra-processed or not. Try to eat without distractions such as the television or your phone, and slow down your eating, keeping a check of your emotions as well as your hunger and fullness levels.

One way to improve mindfulness is to question what you really need in that moment of experiencing strong feelings. Brainstorming *'if ... then'* strategies can be helpful when it comes to emotional eating. This means sitting down with a pen and paper when you're feeling positive or happy, and writing down potential emotions along with possible coping strategies (other than food). For example, *'If* I am feeling lonely, *then* I will phone a friend for a chat', or, *'If* I am feeling angry, *then* I will take myself outside and practise deep breathing' (a simple breathing exercise, called the '4-7-8 technique', involves breathing in for 4 seconds, holding the breath for 7 seconds and exhaling for 8 seconds).

Take time to breathe before making decisions about what to eat. Shorter inhales and longer exhales can stimulate the parasympathetic nervous system, helping us to feel calmer. You may find that your head hunger and heart hunger fade away after around 15 to 20 minutes, whereas stomach hunger would only build in intensity during this time.

Stomach hunger: remember structure and regular meals

Our bodies like routine and regularity, so try to stick to an eating regime that works for you. Different lifestyles and the different ways in which our bodies respond to food mean that there isn't a one size fits all when it comes to finding a suitable eating regime. Some people find that having three regular meals a day works for them, and others require snacks in between. Some people find that skipping breakfast is helpful in their healthy eating pursuits, however the baseline that I usually encourage is to aim for three regular meals a day, with snacks in between meals if needed. If your body is used to this eating pattern, try not to miss meals, as this could lead to excessive stomach hunger, which can drive unplanned UPF consumption.

Balanced meals containing wholegrains, protein and vegetables will keep you satiated and full, and staying adequately hydrated throughout the day will also help. We should be aiming for 6–8 glasses or cups of fluid a day, at least.

Be patient, try different methods and techniques, and if you are still struggling to manage a particular kind of hunger – whether that is head, heart or stomach hunger – then do speak to a dietitian or registered nutritionist for further support.

STARTING YOUR FOOD DIARY

In order to see what changes need to be made, it is useful to see exactly what is going on. When it comes to diet, a food diary can be helpful in turning you into a bit of a diet detective. There is no specific rule when it comes to creating your diary – some people prefer a structured electronic template, whereas others may prefer to use a paper diary. One of my patients used to do a food diary for one week of every month, just to see how he was eating generally, and to keep himself accountable.

Why can food diaries be helpful?

- Food diaries allow you to gain information on your eating habits, and increase your awareness of what causes you to eat – i.e. why you eat and your food triggers.

- Food diaries require mindful engagement with your food intake, and by recording what is eaten and drunk at times of consumption, including details of portion size, any extras and how you may have felt at the time, you gain greater insight into your habits.

- Food diaries help you to be more in tune with your hunger and fullness cues, recognising which foods and meals leave you feeling satiated and which don't.

How to get the most from a food diary

- Record the time as well as the food and drink being consumed – are you eating and drinking regularly?

- Make a note of where you ate and how quickly – were you distracted?

- Reflect on why you ate what you did – what were your emotions before and after?

- Try not to make any conscious changes, instead simply be inquisitive.

- Be as honest as possible with your typical eating habits to get the most out of the process, and to help identify areas you'd like to change. Remember, no one is judging you. This is your opportunity to learn about yourself!

HOW TO START YOUR THREE- TO SEVEN-DAY FOOD DIARY, INCLUDING AT LEAST ONE DAY AT THE WEEKEND

Have a go at recording the foods and drinks that you have over the next three to seven days. There's no right or wrong length of time here, however the more data, the better. You can use whatever methods suit you to record your daily intake, however you may find it useful to re-create the following table to keep track of things.

Make sure to record the time, the foods eaten as well as any thoughts or feelings too, as shown in the example given on Monday.

	Monday	Continue for Tuesday to Sunday
Breakfast	7am: Porridge with berries and honey eaten at home – felt good before and after this (stomach hunger)	
Morning snack	11am: 4 biscuits (UPF) in an office meeting – didn't plan to eat these but head hunger got the better of me	
Lunch	1pm: Brought in a chicken and salad wrap with a yoghurt to the office – ate this quickly at my desk and had some crisps (UPF) from the vending machine	
Afternoon snack	4pm: Brought an apple to eat but didn't fancy it so had a latte instead	
Evening meal	8pm: Lasagne ready meal as was late home from work – convenient UPF. Added my own side salad.	
Dessert/ evening snack	9pm: Ice cream (UPF) from the weekend – felt stressed (heart hunger)	
Drinks	Water – 3 cups Coffee (milk no sugar) – 2 cups Can of diet cola in the afternoon (UPF)	

Don't worry about what to do with the information you gather yet. Instead, as you progress through the next few weeks, use it as a benchmark, and see it as useful data to mull over to see what changes need to be made. We're not going to tackle everything at once (far from it!), as this four-week plan has been designed to take you through each meal and snack time step by step, one week at a time.

Did you know that the majority of people under-report when it comes to talking about what they eat? Sometimes this is down to forgetfulness and mindless eating – we literally forget about the micro-eating moments, such as the biscuit eaten while waiting for the kettle to boil, or the piece of cheese eaten while cooking a meal. Try to capture *everything* that you eat, even in those micro-eating moments, when you are completing your three- to seven-day food diary.

REORGANISING YOUR KITCHEN AND WHY IT'S IMPORTANT

As we progress through the weeks, I will be offering you some helpful hints and tips as to how best to organise the space in which you eat. There are two things that we are trying to achieve here.

1 **Making the healthier choice the easier choice:** it's easy to grab a piece of fruit if it's already washed and in a fruit bowl on the counter. It's easy to eat carrots and hummus if the carrots have been pre-chopped and are placed next to the hummus in the fridge. The aim is to make eating non-UPFs as simple as possible.

2 **Creating 'pause points':** these are moments that allow you to pause and reflect on the food decision that is about to be made. Creating a 'pause point' is as simple as moving the biscuit tin to a shelf that's just out of easy reach, for example. The idea is to reduce the frequency of mindlessly eating UPFs.

If you're eager to get started on this, take a look at your kitchen how it is now, and spend 10 to 15 minutes moving foods around using the following tips:

- **Organise your fridge:** the key is the eye line. You want any less-nutritious UPF foods below the eye line, and more-nutritious food like pre-cut fruit and vegetable sticks and healthy dips at eye-line level. But it is also important to take into account food safety too, so raw meat needs to be on the bottom shelf. With leftover desserts, such as brownies or cake, cover these up with lids and put them somewhere out of the eye line, so that when you want a mid-morning snack you think cucumber and tzatziki rather than cake.

- **Rearrange your cupboards:** move your breakfast cereals so that healthier options like oats and wheat biscuits are front and centre, while less healthy options (think sugar and chocolate coated!) and UPFs are behind. Make sure any less-nutritious UPF snacks, such as sweets and crisps, are in a more inconvenient to access drawer or cupboard.

- **Switch up your work surface:** like the visual eye-line tip for your fridge, put a fruit bowl out on the side, together with a blender for smoothies. Make sure all other foods are in their places in a cupboard or drawer.

ASSESSING THE FOOD THAT'S ALREADY IN YOUR KITCHEN

Before we embark on this four-week plan to reduce your intake of UPFs, it may be helpful to have a look at the ingredients and foods that are in your kitchen right now, then to decide how you can make more-informed choices on what you buy moving forward. Remember, the journey towards reducing UPFs is just that, a journey, and I understand the confusion that can arise when it comes to navigating modern-day foods. To help with this, I've put together a table which can be found on page 266 in the Appendix.

The table in the Appendix categorises foods into four groups according to their level of processing and nutritional value, as discussed in the introduction, and this should serve as a useful roadmap when it comes to stocking a healthier kitchen, providing options for snacks, meals and drinks too.

Groups 1 and 2 represent 'unprocessed' and 'minimally processed' foods. These groups refer to foods that are as close to their natural state as possible – from fresh and frozen fruit and vegetables, to potatoes and wholegrain rice and lean proteins, too. They provide maximum health benefits without unnecessary additives, and should make up the bulk of your fridge and food cupboards.

Groups 3 and 4, on the other hand, are for more processed foods, and are technically classed as UPFs. I've split UPFs into two groups depending on the nutritional value that they hold. UPFs in group 3 provide more in the way of nutrition (based on their macro- and micronutrient makeup) than group 4, which often contain added sugars, unhealthy fats or additives introduced during processing and production. Although all UPFs can still form part of a balanced diet when consumed responsibly (especially the more nutritious UPFs), those in group 4 represent foods that we may need to pause and assess before bringing into our home – is there a more nutritious or non-UPF alternative?

> ### Which oil is best to use?
>
> Oil is a common store cupboard ingredient for any home cook, and oils in the UK are generally considered to be a non-UPF. When it comes to choosing oils for your kitchen, research tells us that olive oil and rapeseed oil (commonly labelled as vegetable oil) are two of the best, thanks to their high unsaturated fat profiles. The label will usually tell you if the oil in question is suitable for low heat (salad dressings and pastas) or high heat (frying). In general, those that are cold-pressed, or darker or greener in colour, aren't as heat stable as those that are refined and more yellow in colour.

HOW DO YOU READ A FOOD LABEL?

Reading a food label is helpful when looking to identify UPFs (both the more-nutritious and less-nutritious types). They can be a little tricky to understand at first, especially as different brands use different ways of highlighting certain nutrients, but here are some key things to consider when reading food labels while you are shopping, either in person or online.

Ingredients list

I always say, 'The ingredients list never lies', and it's true. When someone asks me, 'Is this (packaged) food healthy?', the first thing I do is turn it over to look at the ingredients list, to look at what is actually inside it! Ingredients are listed in order of weight, so the main ingredients in a packaged food always come first.

When it comes to soups for example, I would be checking that foods such as vegetables, beans, lentils or chicken were near the top of the list, with spices further down (as they appear in much smaller quantities for flavour). If sugar is near the top of the ingredients list, for example on a packet of sweets, then you may want to think twice before you buy, just because sugar contains nothing but empty calories – so all you are paying for is energy (oh, and to rot your teeth!).

Regarding common allergens, these will be written in bold (or sometimes in capitals in bakeries) within the ingredients list, e.g. WHEAT and MILK. This is a fairly recent change which means that identifying allergens on the label is easier.

When it comes to identifying UPFs, a long ingredients list can be a giveaway. You want to be on the lookout for foods containing additives added during processing, including emulsifiers* and preservatives (these should be clearly labelled and will likely include sodium benzoate and sodium nitrate), artificial colours and flavour enhancers, as well as thickeners such as modified starches and xanthan gum.

Remember, though, that not all UPFs are created equal, and what matters most is the other ingredients and nutrients that the food in question is providing, in addition to the portion size and frequency with which the food is being eaten.

Traffic light labelling

Colour-coded nutritional information tells you at a glance if the food is high, medium or low in fats (including saturated fats, which we should be eating less of), sugars and salt. Red means

---

* *For more information on emulsifiers, please see page 263 of the Appendix.*

high, amber means medium and green means low. As a general rule, we should be eating more products with greener labels and fewer products with red labels.

If a product is high in fat, sugar or salt, then it may be an indication that the food is also high in calories and could be an energy-dense and less-nutritious UPF; this is particularly true for higher fat products, as fat contains more than twice the number of calories per gram in comparison to carbohydrates (and sugar) and protein (nine calories per gram versus four calories per gram).

What the traffic light label doesn't tell you though is whether any sugar contained in a product has been added or if it is naturally occurring. The traffic light label also doesn't tell you if the food is a UPF or not – only the ingredients list will tell you this. Foods such as tomatoes and dates, for example, contain naturally occurring fruit sugars, and are whole foods (rather than UPFs). As previously explained, it's always best to check the ingredients list to see what you're about to eat.

Foods that tend to be high in salt include salted nuts, crisps, ready meals, fast food, some soups and processed meats. We should aim to eat less than 6g of salt a day (a heaped teaspoon), however keep in mind that 75 per cent of the salt that we eat is already in foods, and many of those foods are ultra-processed.

Nutritional stats

The nutritional label (the numbers in the table!) can be useful when comparing two products; for this I would say to use the 'per 100g' column. It may be useful to compare protein, fibre or salt content, for example, depending on your nutrition goals – foods containing more protein and fibre may be more filling, and foods containing less salt will be better for high blood pressure.

Nutrition claims

Nutrition claims (if a product has them) can be useful to see. For example, it is helpful to know, at a glance, if something is high in protein, whether it contains one of your five a day (we should be eating at least five portions of fruit and vegetables a day; a portion is a handful), if a food is gluten free (pertinent if you have coeliac disease, for example) and/or is suitable for vegans or vegetarians. Nutrition claims are often associated with UPFs, however non-UPFs may also carry claims too. For example, walnuts often say 'high in fibre' on the front.

WHAT ABOUT CALORIES AND UPFs? DO I NEED TO PAY ATTENTION TO THEM?

Calories (i.e. energy) in food are measured using a 'bomb calorimeter' in which the temperature rise of the water is used to calculate the number of calories contained within a specific food. The caloric availability of foods (the amount of energy we digest, absorb and metabolise) depends on a number of factors though, and there are two particular nutrients, protein and fibre, that are digested more slowly, meaning it takes more energy for our body to metabolise these in comparison to simple carbohydrates and fats.

What this means is two things: firstly, the calorie content on the back of the packet is likely to be inaccurate (potentially by up to 20 per cent); and secondly, the more processed a food, the more calories we are likely to be able to extract from it. A useful comparison is a handful of almonds (full of healthy fats, some protein and fibre too) versus a chocolate bar – both may contain a similar number of calories, but the calories in the chocolate bar will be more available to us due to the high level of processing and the higher sugar content, too.

If we are in an energy deficit (i.e. exerting more energy than we are consuming), we will experience weight loss, however this doesn't necessarily mean better health. For example, if someone eats (approximately) 1500 calories (kcal) of UPFs that are lacking in essential nutrients such as vitamins, minerals, fibre and protein, they will lose weight, but their health will suffer and their energy levels may be compromised too.

When it comes to calories, we need to think more about food quality than quantity. So, although for some people calorie counting can be a short-term approach to managing weight, we could instead consider:

- ensuring we're getting our five a day (5 × 80g portions of fruit and vegetables a day)

- consuming the recommended daily amount of fibre (30g a day)

- increasing non-UPF protein to keep well satiated (through both animal and plant sources, depending on our dietary preferences)

- making sure the predominant type of fat in our diet is unsaturated

- including foods that we enjoy and make us feel good in moderation too!

- eating fewer UPFs overall.

Are vitamins UPFs?

Vitamins are not a UPF, as they are classed as supplements. Without knowing you personally it is hard to say whether this is definitely the case for you or not, but in general, we should be able to get most of the nutrients we need from the food we eat, with the exception of 10mcg of vitamin D in the winter months (or all year round if you are pregnant, breastfeeding or susceptible to deficiency). If you are following a vegan lifestyle, the main supplements you may want to look into taking are calcium, iodine, vitamin B12 and omega-3 (based on algae), as well as iron and selenium. Folic acid (usually 400mcg) should also be taken before and during pregnancy. Vitamin and mineral supplements are not substitutes for a healthy and balanced diet, as they do not provide fibre or other phytochemicals (healthy plant nutrients).

SOME PROCESSED AND ULTRA-PROCESSED FOOD MYTH-BUSTING!

Before we embark on your four-week plan, I thought it best to do some myth-busting for the most prolific processed and ultra-processed foods. Let's set the record straight on some of the noise I've heard in both traditional media and social media over recent times.

Food/ drink item	Common myth	The truth
Almond butter	It's significantly healthier than peanut butter	Both almond butter and peanut butter provide similar amounts of calories, unsaturated fats, protein and fibre. Both should be eaten in relative moderation due to the fat content. Ideally choose varieties with no added salt or sugar. Most nut butters are not classed as UPFs.
Coconut oil	It's a superfood and is healthier than other fats	Coconut oil is high in saturated fats, which isn't the preferred fat for health (unsaturated fat is preferred). It can be used in moderation, but it's not necessarily healthier than other oils like olive oil. It is certainly not recommended to eat spoonfuls of coconut oil, or to add it to your coffee! Save it for the right curry, and use it conservatively. Oils are not usually classed as UPFs.
Diet soda/ fizzy drink	They're just as bad for health as regular sugary fizzy drinks	Diet fizzy drinks don't contain sugar, and are therefore better for preventing high blood sugar levels than the regular equivalent. The sweeteners used in diet drinks are safe for consumption, as previously discussed, but diet drinks are far from being 'health drinks', and they do not have positive effects on teeth. Water, including sparkling, with no-added-sugar squash and tea are better choices, however social circumstances will dictate which drink you choose when. Remember, frequency of consumption matters, and it isn't about avoiding ultra-processed drinks altogether.

Food/drink item	Common myth	The truth
Frozen vegetables	They're less nutritious than fresh vegetables	Frozen vegetables are classed as minimally processed, and are picked and frozen at peak ripeness, preserving their nutritional value. In some cases, they may even retain nutrients better than fresh vegetables that have been transported and stored for long periods of time. The same applies to frozen fruits too.
Gluten-free foods	They're healthier for everyone	Pre-packaged gluten-free foods are almost all ultra-processed (as gluten is a protein that acts as a natural binder, so it must be replaced with something else in gluten-free products), and the only people who need to have them are those with coeliac disease or a gluten sensitivity. Just like with vegan foods, gluten-free foods are not always healthier and can sometimes be higher in sugars and fats than their gluten-containing equivalents.

Food/ drink item	Common myth	The truth
Granola	It's always a healthy breakfast option	The issue with most shop-bought granolas is that they are UPFs and can be high in added sugars and fats (oils), which means that portion size is the key to enjoying them in a healthy manner. I personally encourage my patients to enjoy (ideally non-UPF) granola as a yoghurt or cereal topper, rather than a cereal base. If you have the time, it's always best to make your own with oats and mixed nuts so you can control the amount of sugar being added. You can always add dried fruits such as dates and apricots to sweeten things up, with the benefit of added fibre and antioxidants, too.
Oat milk	The oils on the ingredients list are inflammatory	Oat milk is a dairy alternative, but it's not a nutritional equivalent to dairy due to its relatively low protein content and low mineral content if not fortified (organic plant-based milks are not fortified). Contrary to belief (and online scaremongering!) though, the oils found in UK oat milk are not inflammatory and in addition are present in relatively small amounts. Always check the label of milk-alternatives to see if it has added calcium, and ideally iodine too, so you don't miss out on nutrients from dairy (iodine is found in dairy and also in white fish).

Food/drink item	Common myth	The truth
Orange juice	It's a UPF and should be avoided at all costs	100 per cent orange juice is not, in fact, a UPF, and 150ml counts as a portion of one of your five a day (even if you have more than 150ml of juice it still counts as just one of your five a day). Having said this though, fruit juice does lack some of the fibre that's found in whole oranges, meaning that it is easy to overconsume. Eating the whole fruit provides more nutritional benefits, including more fibre, so will keep you feeling fuller for longer, but 100 per cent fresh fruit juice does not need to be avoided in my book.
Processed red meats	They're a healthy protein source	Processed red meats do provide protein, however they are often high in both salt and fat too. High intakes have been linked to an increased risk of bowel (colorectal) cancer, which is why the NHS advises people to have no more than 70g a day (or 490g of cooked red or processed meats a week). Processed red meat includes ham, pepperoni, sausages* and bacon, and these are often classed as UPFs too. I would recommend having a mix of non-UPF plant-based as well as animal-based proteins, such as fresh lean meats, fish, beans and legumes, which are healthier. *Some butcher's sausages are not classed as UPF as they do not contain additives, but they are still regarded as processed red meat.

Food/ drink item	Common myth	The truth
Vegan snack alternatives, e.g. biscuits, confectionery and cakes	They're healthier because they're vegan	Vegan doesn't automatically mean healthy. Vegan 'junk foods' may still be classed as UPFs, and can still be high in calories, sugars, salt and unhealthy fats, in addition to containing additives for texture and flavour too. Be aware of 'health halos', as previously discussed.

SETTING YOUR INTENTIONS FOR THE FOUR-WEEK PLAN

Your *why* is going to be the driver of all your decisions. Before you start the plan, write down all of the benefits you will get from making healthier food choices and reducing your UPF intake, as well as where you want to be in a year's time – this is called visualisation, and it can be helpful in maintaining motivation. Here are some example reasons for reducing UPFs:

- To improve my gut health and reduce bloating (I need to eat more fibre!)

- To reduce my spending on impulse purchases when out

- To help me to achieve my five a day (I need space for more nutritious foods!)

- To feel more energised throughout the day.

And here is an example of what you could write for who you want to be in a year's time:

I want to be someone who prioritises what they eat, and has a low intake of UPFs (in particular the less-nutritious

UPFs). I want to feel good about myself, and to have the energy to work out and perform at my best.

Are you ready? Let's go!

A note on eating disorders

If you find yourself preoccupied with food, feel really scared or ashamed that you have gained weight, or if you engage in restrictive, binge or secret eating – it could be worth seeking professional help. Our relationship with food is a complex one and I encourage anyone who exhibits these behaviours or has these thoughts to seek support. Eating disorders and disordered eating can impact anyone, and it's important to pick up early signs as soon as possible. BEAT is the UK's leading eating disorder charity and it offers lots of types of support, from a telephone helpline to resources and online support groups. Speak to your doctor and/or find more information at www.beateatingdisorders.org.uk

---

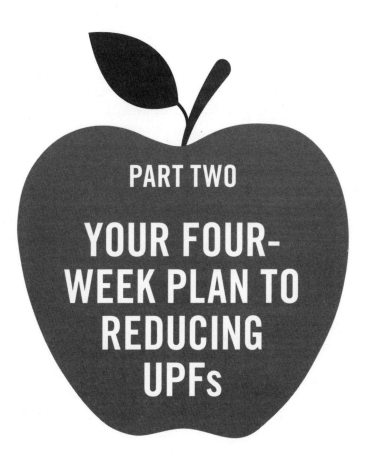

PART TWO

YOUR FOUR-WEEK PLAN TO REDUCING UPFs

CHAPTER 4

DAY ONE – MEAL PLANNING

O n the first day of each week, set time aside to have a think about the week ahead. What meals would you like to eat when, given your prior commitments? Having a meal plan helps to create structure and gives you a clear, bird's eye view of your (planned) dietary intake.

The following blank meal planner offers a template for you to recreate, and although at the end of each chapter I will show you an example of how to incorporate some of the foods, drinks and meals mentioned, this planner is flexible and has been designed so that *you* can take control of *your* nutrition.

You will see that each day has two snacks and an option for a third snack or a dessert. You might not need two snacks and a dessert every day, but they are there just in case. There are no times on this meal planner, as that is dependent on you, your circumstances and your day ahead. My advice is to honour your hunger and fullness cues and focus on balance.

Furthermore, please do not think that every meal needs to be new or extravagant – feel free to batch-cook meals and snacks so they can be repeated throughout the week. If you make a big batch of healthy chilli, for example, why not serve it one evening with rice, and the next with a jacket potato and salad?

Have a go at planning your meals ahead now, or if you prefer to wait until the end of week 1, that is OK too.

	Mon	Tue	Wed	Thu	Fri	Sat	Sun
Breakfast							
Morning snack							
Lunch							
Afternoon snack							
Evening meal							
Dessert/ evening snack							
Drinks							

CHAPTER 5

WEEK 1 – SNACKS AND DRINKS

We're starting with snacks and drinks, as in my clinic I often see these as the 'little wins that can lead to big results'. This is because making changes to snacks and drinks often requires (relatively) little effort, but due to the number of them that may be consumed across the week, this simple change can have a big impact on overall dietary intake. UPFs can feature heavily in people's snack cupboards and drawers (at home and in the office too!) so let's tackle these initially. We'll look at drinks second, for no particular reason other than I love a good snack.

WHAT ACTUALLY IS SNACKING?

The Oxford English Dictionary defines snacking as 'a small amount of food eaten between meals'. Snacking is often seen as a bad thing, but as a dietitian I'm a big fan of (healthy) snacks as they can help to manage stomach hunger (as discussed in Chapter 3), blood glucose (sugar) levels and energy levels. When chosen well, snacks can also help individuals meet not only their five a day, but their daily fibre intake, too.

A snack between meals isn't a bad thing, especially if you rinse your mouth with water afterwards (a tip that I learnt from a dentist!), but 'grazing' is another story. The term grazing is used to describe eating small amounts of food frequently, at random times of the day. There are usually short gaps between each 'graze' and often people either don't remember what they've grazed on that day, or the grazing episodes are not planned. Snacking, on the other hand, is a more planned and purposeful eating episode – some people may even call it a 'mini meal'.

I once met a patient who had completed a one-week food diary as a part of one of my diabetes education sessions. I hadn't asked to look at it, as I wanted her to reflect on any changes that she could make. When I asked her how it went, she told me that she had found it stressful. It turns out that it was stressful because she was grazing for most of the day, all throughout the week. There was no real mealtime structure, and she was under the impression that she wasn't eating a lot. As it turns out though, grazers can often eat more calories and UPFs than their meal- and snack-eating counterparts, because grazing often isn't very filling, which can lead to a dysregulation in hunger and fullness cues and a dissatisfaction with the foods being eaten, thus leading to further food-seeking behaviours and eating episodes.

This example illustrates the importance of mindful eating and establishing structured mealtimes, but it also emphasises that you should eat when you are hungry, rather than just out of habit. So, how do you eat mindfully? Well, have you ever been to an expensive restaurant? I bet you didn't wolf the food down. You will have looked at (and hopefully admired!) the food, smelt it and savoured each bite. This is the mindset we should have when eating. Focusing on snacks high in protein and fibre (think nuts, fruit and even yoghurt), and planning them into your week, can make all the difference to your relationship with food and how you feel too.

NON-UPF SNACKS VERSUS MORE- AND LESS-NUTRITIOUS UPF SNACKS

UPF snacks exist everywhere – from the supermarkets to service stations, local shops to cafes. In fact, it's quite hard to find anywhere that doesn't sell them! That's thanks not only to their long shelf life, but also because they sell – most UPF snacks are easy to eat and taste good, there's no denying that! Even worse is the ratio of less-nutritious UPF snacks to more-nutritious UPF snacks – I can't tell you the number of times I've been fuelling up my car between clinics and have wanted to grab something relatively healthy (if I've forgotten to bring something with me), yet have been faced with row after row of sugar-laden snacks that do nothing for nutritional intake or energy, never mind teeth!

As discussed in the introduction, foods can be viewed on a processing and nutritional scale (as shown in the following table), and it's up to you to decide which column you want to be eating from most. I'm guessing, as you're reading a book about how to eat fewer UPFs, that you would like to move to eating more of the snacks on the left-hand side, in comparison to those on the right. As a dietitian, I would suggest eating mostly non-UPF snacks, some more-nutritious UPF snacks, and fewer of the less-nutritious UPF snacks.

Non-UPF snack examples	More-nutritious or less energy-dense UPF snack examples	Less-nutritious or more energy-dense UPF snack examples
Homemade snack bar made with dried fruit, nuts, oats and optional plain dark chocolate* (at least 70 per cent cocoa)	Packaged snack bar that contains dried fruit, nuts or oats (in addition to ingredients not usually found in a home kitchen)	Packaged chocolate bar with caramel or milk chocolate
Shop-bought energy bites containing only whole foods	Dark chocolate-coated almonds	Boiled sweets
Chopped carrots with hummus (non-UPF shop bought or homemade)	Energy bites, main ingredients being date paste, cashews and almonds	Packaged pastries or long-life cakes or flapjacks (first ingredient being sugar)
Rye crackers with cottage cheese and cucumber or oatcakes with nut butter and sliced banana or berries	Small bag of popcorn (ideally non sugar coated) or banana chips	Crisps (most are UPFs)

---

* *Dark chocolate is still high in fat and sugar so should be consumed in moderation.*

HOW TO CHOOSE BETWEEN TWO UPF SNACKS

Let's look at the ingredients lists and nutritional differences between two of the UPF examples shown in the table that you'd find in a supermarket: boiled sweets and chocolate-coated almonds.

Boiled sweets provide very little in the way of any nutrients, as their main ingredient is sugar. When I looked up the ingredients of some 'mint humbugs' available in my local supermarket though, I was quite surprised, as it read:

> **Supermarket mint humbug ingredients** – *Glucose Syrup, Sugar, Palm Oil, Condensed Skimmed Milk, Invert Sugar Syrup, Colour (Plain Caramel), Butteroil (Milk), Salt, Flavourings, Emulsifier (Lecithins).*

In comparison, a very well-known 'healthy' brand's chocolate almonds, also available in the same supermarket, contain:

> **Dark chocolate-coated almonds ingredients** – *Dark Chocolate (60%) (Cocoa Mass, Sugar, Cocoa Butter, Emulsifier (Soya Lecithin), Natural Vanilla Flavouring), Almonds (39%), Salt, Cocoa Powder.*

These examples show how processed snacks can vary drastically in their nutritional profile. The chocolate almonds provide an abundance of healthy fats, protein and fibre from the almonds, as well as antioxidants from the cocoa. The chocolate almonds would therefore leave you feeling much fuller than the boiled sweets. So, while a homemade, non-UPF snack will always be the optimal choice, it's nice to know that if we are caught hungry, without a homemade snack to hand, there are better choices that can be made.

Food is more than just the calories and macronutrients it provides, and the ingredients list is more important than the nutrition label. Food quality matters.

Before we move on, let's also compare a standard milk chocolate bar (a UPF example), with some plain dark chocolate (a non-UPF example) – just to encourage you to do this with your own snacks!

Milk chocolate ingredients – *Milk, Sugar, Cocoa Butter, Cocoa Mass, Vegetable Fats (Palm, Shea), Emulsifiers (E442, E476), Flavourings.*

Dark chocolate (70% cocoa) ingredients – *Cocoa Mass, Sugar, Cocoa Butter, Vanilla.*

Ingredients are placed in order of how much of each ingredient the product contains, with the ingredient present in the largest quantity listed first, so as you can see from this example, the dark chocolate contains just four ingredients (all of which you could find in a home kitchen), in comparison to the milk chocolate bar, which contains seven (three of which would not normally be found at home: fat – palm and shea; emulsifiers; and flavourings).

There's no comparison with regards to which chocolate bar is quite obviously ultra-processed versus the one that is not, so keep the ingredients list in mind the next time you're buying chocolate, and as always, try to moderate the portion size and frequency with which you consume it. Choose lower-sugar and higher-fibre snacks for the majority of the time, or add some healthy fats and protein in the form of dried fruit and nuts to chocolate to make a healthier trail mix.

If you're not keen on 70 per cent dark chocolate, try to gradually increase the percentage of cocoa that you buy. Many chocolate bars labelled as 'dark chocolate' typically contain around 50 per cent cocoa and these are a good place to start.

WHAT ARE THE COMMON PROBLEMS WITH UPF SNACKS?

Many of our favourite UPF snacks, like sweets, chocolate bars, crisps and pastries, lack essential nutrients as well as protein and fibre, and as such their satiety values are often questionable. This means that although they may taste good, they don't do much for our physical health, or mental health for that matter, and could lead to further food cravings just a short time after eating. UPF snacks are extremely easy and relatively quick to consume, which means that you can be mindlessly eating a UPF snack without really realising what you're doing. If you've ever eaten at your desk, how many times have you started eating your favourite UPF snack, only to be distracted with work, and then the next minute you've finished the snack but don't quite remember the last few bites, and don't feel in the least bit satisfied?

Food isn't 'good' or 'bad' though, and as a pretty grounded dietitian I pride myself on being realistic – cutting out chocolate bars and crisps (i.e. less-nutritious UPFs) forever isn't realistic, which is why I advocate cutting down as much as possible (80 per cent of the time, at least), and making healthy swaps for the most part. This means planning to have healthy, filling and nutritious snacks most of the time that are ideally non-UPF, but if some more-nutritious UPF snacks creep in then so be it, as it's what your diet looks like the majority of the time that matters most. This is the beauty of the 80/20 rule – if you plan to eat healthily 80 per cent of the time, when 'life happens' you have the flexibility to cope with it and it won't affect your health. Take a colleague's birthday, for example: while you may not have planned to have chocolate cake that day, you can have some and enjoy it without it impacting on your health goals, because the rest of your diet allows for it.

> Focus on what you should be eating more of, and you will naturally eat fewer of the foods that you should be eating less of. This means focusing your efforts on eating more non-UPF snacks, which will leave less room for those pesky less-nutritious UPF snacks!

Another issue with UPF snacks is their environmental impact. These foods are often wrapped in single-use plastic that goes straight to landfill, so choosing whole, minimally processed foods is better for the planet, too. Many of the more-nutritious UPF brands are also more environmentally conscious. This means that a lot of their packaging may be made from paper and can be recycled.

TOP TIPS TO MAKE SNACK TIME LESS ABOUT UPFs AND MUCH MORE NUTRITIOUS

When it comes to taking those first important steps to consuming fewer UPFs at snack time, let's first work out *how often* they are creeping in, which you can do by taking a look at your food diary. Ask yourself – is it once an hour, once a day or once a week? You then want to look at where the snacks are being eaten, as this will influence what kind of changes you'll want to make. For example, are you home when most of the snacking is done (if so, do we need to look at your kitchen?), or are you on the go (do you need to prepare and take healthy snacks with you?), or are the UPF snacks creeping in at work (if so, this may require some rearranging of where they're accessed from, which we will come on to!)?

Here are some of my top tips to consider adopting when it comes to making snack time less about UPFs and much more nutritious:

- **Read the food label:** as we've discussed, the ingredients list never lies. Choose snacks that are based around nuts, fruit and oats for more fibre, protein and healthy fats, too. In general, the fewer ingredients, the better, but a long ingredients list shouldn't automatically be dismissed. Take a wholegrain breakfast cereal, for example – the ingredients list will be made longer if it has added vitamins and minerals (see the Appendix for more information).

- **Think protein and produce:** when it comes to making your own snacks, think about adding a source of both protein and fibre. This will not only increase satiety and nutrient intake, but satisfaction too. For example, try hummus with carrots, or yoghurt with berries.

- **Add one of your five a day:** in clinic, I always tell my patients to ask 'where is the colour' when it comes to their snacks, and to add at least one portion of fruit and vegetables – for example, sliced banana on an oatcake with nut butter. Colours mean antioxidants and polyphenols (healthy plant chemicals).

- **Prep once, eat twice:** when you want to make a healthy snack, make sure to double up on the ingredients so you can eat one portion now and one the following day – hummus is a great one for this, and homemade snack bars can be made ten at a time (see my recipe for No-bake fruit and oat bars on page 90).

- **Invest in on-the-go containers and reusable snack bags:** these make homemade snacks more desirable (and environmentally friendly) to take with you on the go.

- **Set up a healthy snack rota:** if you work in an office, you could take it in turns with a few colleagues to bring in healthy snacks on one day of the week. This adds both accountability and support, and is a great way of discovering new healthy recipes and healthier-UPF snack brands too. It's easier to change habits when you feel supported.

HEALTHY NON-UPF SNACK IDEAS

If you're going to reduce the number of UPFs that you're eating at snack time, it's a good idea to have some unprocessed snack ideas in your toolkit. I've listed ten of my favourites here. Most of them can be transported easily in little tubs, food bags or a mini-cool bag if you're going to be on the road for most of the day, and all of them can be made up quickly. If you have more time, then check out the recipes shown at the end of this section for some healthy suggestions, including homemade energy balls, and snack bars that you can make in bulk and take with you as needed.

1 **Roasted chickpeas:** simply rinse and dry tinned chickpeas, season with your favourite herbs and a little olive oil and roast in the oven until crunchy (takes about 25 minutes).

2 **Carrots and hummus:** if you're buying shop-bought hummus, look for one with the least ingredients (for reference, an average tub of hummus contains around seven ingredients including water), and if you want to make it yourself, check out the recipes at the end of this section. Choosing low-fat or full-fat hummus is a personal choice – depending on which option leaves you feeling more satisfied!

3 **Apple and cheese:** what's not to love about this crunchy and cheesy option?! I usually suggest sticking to around 30g per serving of cheese (around the size of a small match box).

4 **Berries and plain yoghurt:** a delicious combination of vitamins, fibre and protein too. Feel free to add some seeds and a little honey if desired, or change the fruit choice.

5 **Dried fruit and nuts:** the ideal protein and produce snack. To make this snack a little more interesting, you could make a healthy trail mix using your favourite plain nuts (raw or toasted), dried fruit and some plain popcorn and dark chocolate too.

6 **Plain popcorn:** pop your own at home using popping corn for a tasty source of wholegrain and fibre too. Season with a touch of sea salt if desired.

7 **Oatcakes with peanut butter and sliced pear:** easy to make, packed with soluble fibre and healthy fats, and super versatile.

8 **Rye crackers with cottage cheese and cucumber:** a lovely crunch with great flavour, providing wholegrains, protein and one of your five a day, too.

9 **Medjool dates with nut butter and a square or two of dark chocolate:** ideal if you have a sweet tooth, this snack is loaded with healthy fats and fibre.

10 **Hard-boiled egg with avocado on a crisp bread:** the perfect savoury option, packed with protein, fibre and healthy fats.

Remember, if you fail to plan, you plan to fail! Supermarkets, local shops and petrol stations are known for their high-UPF offerings and fast foods, so bringing some healthier (non-UPF) snacks, or knowing how to read an ingredients list, is key to sticking to your nutrition goals in a high-UPF environment.

SHOPPING LIST EASY WINS – YOUR KITCHEN ESSENTIALS FOR HEALTHY SNACKS

Having a basic supply of healthy ingredients in your kitchen is fundamental when it comes to being able to prepare healthy snacks either for on the go or to have at home. Have a look in your kitchen at what's available in comparison to the following list – which items do you need to add to your next shopping list? You don't need to buy all of these items, especially if you have any food allergies, intolerances or strong dislikes. They are here simply for inspiration.

Fresh produce and fridge items

- **Apples, bananas and oranges** are ideal quick snacks that provide vitamins and fibre, which will keep you feeling full.

- **Carrots, cucumbers, celery and bell peppers** make great dippers for tzatziki and hummus when chopped – keep them in a sealed container for freshness.

- **Hummus and tzatziki** are refreshing dips with higher protein. They can be homemade, too.

- **Fresh berries** are great to add to yoghurt.

- **Avocados** are handy to add to crackers for a source of healthy fats for hair and skin.

- **Eggs** can be hard-boiled in advance to provide an easy, protein-rich snack option.

- **Plain yoghurt** or Greek yoghurt has more protein (remember, that friendly bacteria, i.e. live cultures, listed on the ingredients list does not make it a UPF).

Full-fat or fat-free yoghurt?

I'm often asked if fat free, low fat or full fat is best when it comes to dairy, and the truth is that it's dependent on a few things – namely portion size, preference and what the rest of the diet looks like. Choosing a plain yoghurt (one that you can sweeten yourself naturally at home with fruit or even honey) will always be best, and I often advise my patients to choose a reduced-fat plain yoghurt (or semi-skimmed milk) as a happy medium, as it is a good source of protein and calcium too. If you prefer eating by volume, perhaps fat-free plain yoghurt may be best for you. Equally though, if you enjoy the richness of a full-fat plain yoghurt, choose that, but make sure to moderate the portion size and include some nuts or seeds for some healthy unsaturated fats elsewhere in the diet too.

Cupboard items

- **No-added-sugar muesli or granola (non-UPF option)** to add to yoghurt (cereal isn't just for breakfast!). Or have a go at making your own 'raw' granola by crumbling up the homemade snack bars in the recipe part of this section before chilling.

- **Nuts**, such as almonds, walnuts, Brazil nuts, cashews or mixed nuts (plain).

- **Seeds**, such as sunflower, pumpkin, sesame or chia (mix these into a jar as an ideal plant-based topper for yoghurt).

- **Dried fruit**, such as dried apricots, raisins and dates add natural sweetness to your day, which can help when you are feeling tempted by a chocolate biscuit.

- **Nut butters** (peanut, almond or cashew) are perfect for dipping fruit into, or for spreading on crackers, rice cakes or toast.

- **Dark chocolate** can be grated onto yoghurt or melted into baking; for optimal healthiness select varieties with a higher cocoa content (ideally 70 per cent or more).

- **Wholegrain or rye crackers** are a great base for versatile toppings.

- **Popcorn kernels** to air-pop for a fibre-rich snack, or choose the simpler, more plain packaged popcorns (compare the ingredients lists and choose the one with the fewest ingredients).

- **Oats** are seen as more of a breakfast item, but they are handy for making healthy snacks like oat bars and for bulking out smoothies.

- **Chickpeas** (dried or tinned) are also worth having in your cupboard to make hummus with (see page 85 for my recipe for Healthy hummus – four ways). Just make sure, if you are buying the dried varieties, to soak and cook them the day before.

- **Tinned tuna, salmon and mackerel** to put on crackers, toast or cucumber slices. Choose varieties tinned in spring water or tomatoes, or drain well if tinned with salt or oil.

Frozen foods

- **Frozen fruits** can be added to yoghurt and can be used in baking too.

- **Frozen edamame beans** are great for a tasty snack. Simply grab a handful, plunge into boiling water or microwave according to the instructions on the packet, drain, then sprinkle with sea salt – popping them in the oven or air-fryer is an optional extra step to crisp them up!

HOW TO ORGANISE YOUR SPACES FOR HEALTHIER SNACKING

You might have decluttered your wardrobe, but what about your kitchen? The aim is to make the healthy choice the easy choice – this is essential when your will power is depleted after a hard day.

In the kitchen

- Make pre-cut crudités and store in sealed containers at eye level in the fridge next to healthy dips such as salsa, hummus and tzatziki (either homemade or shop bought).

- Stock up your fruit bowl with your favourite fruits.

- Move the biscuit tin to a more inconvenient location, i.e. not next to the kettle.

- Move any less-nutritious UPF snacks into opaque containers and put them in a more inconvenient location.

- Store healthier snacks in clear containers in an easy-to-access cupboard.

In the office

- Suggest that all food items, including birthday cake and buns, are kept in the kitchen area, or at the very least on a table that isn't in your eye line.

- Make sure any of your less-nutritious UPF snack foods are kept in the kitchen.

- Keep only non-UPF or more-nutritious UPF foods in your desk drawers.

- Have a box at work into which you can put recipe cards for healthy snacks to share ideas with your colleagues.

In the car

- Remove all less-nutritious UPF snacks (and wrappers!) and keep them in the house (they will be less tempting there).

- Keep more-nutritious UPF snacks in the boot for emergency snacking.

- Invest in a mini cool-bag and an ice pack if you're on the road a lot, as well as mini storage containers for homemade healthy snacks.

MEAL PLANNER WITH NON-UPF SNACKS

Snacks are often forgotten about when it comes to meal planning, and as a result we can instead be prone to the spontaneous buying of UPFs. I've included a suggested meal plan in this chapter, complete with some of the snack ideas mentioned earlier to cater for different tastes and dietary needs.

The aim of having a meal plan is to avoid mindless eating, and to instead put some thought into what is being eaten when. Whether you're looking for something quick and easy, a sweet treat that doesn't derail your health goals, or a savoury option to satisfy those afternoon cravings, this planner has got you covered.

I understand that people want variety, however if you don't mind eating the same snacks each day, it's a good idea to make a big batch of the right recipes and eat these more than once to save time.

This planner, complete with healthy snack ideas, is not encouraging you to eat between meals if you are *not* hungry, rather it's there to give suggested options in case you *do* become hungry, or if a meal is going to be delayed for whatever reason.

	Monday	Tuesday	Wednesday
Breakfast			
Morning snack	Apple and cheese	Oatcakes topped with nut butter and banana slices	Berries with plain yoghurt and a drizzle of honey if desired
Lunch			
Afternoon snack	Carrots and hummus – homemade (see recipe on page 85) or shop bought	Dark chocolate and coconut energy balls (see recipe on page 88)	Small bag of popcorn – or pop at home with kernels
Evening meal			
Dessert/ evening snack			
Drinks			

Thursday	Friday	Saturday	Sunday
Healthy trail mix – made from plain nuts, dried fruit and dark chocolate	Dried apricots and almonds	Medjool dates stuffed with nut butter and a little dark chocolate	Avocado on a wholegrain cracker with slices of boiled egg
Roasted butter beans with olive oil and spices	No-bake fruit and oat bars (see recipe on page 90)	Pear and a handful of walnuts	Roasted kale crisps

YOUR FIVE-STEP HEALTHY CHECKLIST
FOR WEEK 1 (SNACKS)

Goals are best achieved when they are broken down into steps. So, if your overall goal is to reduce your intake of UPF snacks, you need to think about how exactly you are going to achieve this. In the following table are some examples of goals you could focus on for the week and month ahead (everyone works at their own rate, and that is OK). Think about which of these goals resonate with you, or those that you'd find easy to do, and start with those (or come up with your own goals). Make it easy to win, as success builds confidence, which leads to more action and more success!

Tick on the left if you want to work on a particular goal, and on the right when you have achieved it:

Week 1 – snacks and drinks

Tick to work on ✔	Goal	Tick when completed ✔
	Plan your mealtimes, and when a healthy snack may be needed, e.g. mid-morning or mid-afternoon, after work or in the evening.	
	Make a list of the top five healthy snacks that you could make at home – think protein and produce and use the examples in this section for inspiration.	
	Rearrange your kitchen so a healthy choice is the easy choice, e.g. move the biscuit tin and make sure the chopped crudités are in the fridge with healthy dips such as hummus, as discussed earlier.	
	Choose a new or seasonal fruit or vegetable and create a snack around it, e.g. put it on an oatcake with nut butter or have it with yoghurt.	
	Work out how many UPF snacks you have a day or in a week and swap at least one or two for a more nutritious UPF snack, or ideally a homemade (non-UPF) snack.	

NON-UPF HEALTHY SNACK RECIPES

Before we move on to drinks (which hopefully will be relatively easy to change before we move to week 2), here are three of my favourite non-UPF healthy snack recipes. Choose one or two and give them a go when you have a free moment.

- Healthy hummus – four ways

- Dark chocolate and coconut energy balls

- No-bake fruit and oat bars

HEALTHY HUMMUS – FOUR WAYS

Vegan • **Makes:** 4 portions • **Prep time:** 10 minutes

Homemade hummus is a simple high-protein, high-fibre snack – the perfect dip for everything from vegetable crudités, to homemade wholemeal tortilla chips and warm pitta slices. It is also incredibly versatile: you can switch up the base (for example, you could swap the chickpeas for cannellini beans), explore different flavours by adding a range of plant-based ingredients and add a host of toppings (you could add a sprinkling of seeds or roasted chickpeas, for example) for extra texture, healthy fats and nutrients.

Benefits: Chickpeas are an affordable source of plant-based protein, fibre, iron and folate.

For the classic hummus base recipe
400g tin chickpeas, drained and thoroughly rinsed
60g tahini (sesame seed paste)
1–2 tbsp lemon juice, to taste
2 garlic cloves, minced
2 tbsp olive oil
Salt, to taste
2–4 tbsp cold water (as needed for desired consistency)

For optional additional flavours

1. *Roasted red pepper hummus*

   Add approximately 65g roasted red peppers (drained if from a jar, or you can roast the peppers at home), an additional garlic clove (minced) and a pinch of smoked paprika, as desired.

2. *Avocado, coriander and lime hummus*

   Add 1 ripe avocado, 1–2 tablespoons of freshly chopped
      coriander leaves and lime juice, to taste.
   Note: *this flavoured hummus is best eaten on the same day,
      as the avocado will turn brown.*

3. *Sun-dried tomato and basil hummus*

   Add 120g sun-dried tomatoes (in oil, drained, or reserve
      2 tablespoons of the tomatoes' oil and use instead of the
      olive oil), 15g fresh basil leaves and an extra tablespoon
      of tahini.

4. *Beetroot and mint hummus*

   Add 1 medium-sized cooked beetroot, 2 tablespoons of fresh
      mint leaves (chopped) and 1 tablespoon of lemon juice.

   To serve (optional)
   Smoked paprika, to taste
   Olive oil, to drizzle
   Sesame seeds or roasted chickpeas, for sprinkling
      on top
   Crudités, homemade tortilla chips or sliced pitta,
      for dipping

1. In a food processor, add the chickpeas, tahini, lemon juice,
   garlic, olive oil and a pinch of salt. Blend until almost smooth.

2. Add your chosen flavour (optional – see the options listed
   in the Ingredients section) or continue to step 3 for a classic
   hummus.

3. Gradually add the water, 1 tablespoon at a time, blending
   until you reach your desired consistency.

4. Taste and adjust the lemon juice and salt, as necessary.

5. Spoon into a bowl, lightly dust with paprika (optional) and drizzle with a swirl of olive oil (optional). Serve with crudités, homemade tortilla chips or sliced pitta.

Storage: Cover and chill in the fridge for up to four days, or freeze for up to three months. It is best to drizzle the surface with olive oil before covering and chilling.

DARK CHOCOLATE AND COCONUT ENERGY BALLS

Vegan • **Makes:** 10–12 balls • **Prep time:** 10 minutes
Chill time: 30 minutes

These are one of my go-to snacks when I am craving something sweet but want something more nutritious than a biscuit (which, of course, has its place – everything in moderation!). Make this recipe your own by swapping the almonds for hazelnuts or by experimenting with various nut butters. For extra flavour, toast the desiccated coconut and leave to cool completely before decorating. If you are not a fan of desiccated coconut, you can leave the energy balls undecorated, or you could roll them in chopped almonds instead.

Benefits: These balls contain healthy fats and vitamin E. The combination of nuts, oats and dates provide slow-release energy, and thanks to the fibre content, will help keep you satisfied for longer.

For the energy balls
100g almonds (or ground almonds)
*50g good-quality dark chocolate, at least 70% cocoa solids
(or chocolate chips)*
10g jumbo oats
75g pitted dates
40g almond butter
1–2 tbsp maple syrup, to taste

To decorate
About 25g desiccated coconut (optional, but recommended)

1. Line a baking tray with non-stick baking paper and set aside.

2. Tip the almonds into a food processor and blend until you have a crumb-like consistency (skip this step if you are using ground almonds). Add the dark chocolate and oats and blend again until you have the consistency of breadcrumbs.

3. Add the dates, almond butter and 1 tablespoon of maple syrup. Pulse to combine. Taste to check the sweetness and add a little more maple syrup, if desired, before pulsing again to combine. Tip into a bowl.

4. Sprinkle the baking tray with desiccated coconut in an even layer, if using.

5. Shape the mix into 10–12 balls weighing about 25–30g each. Roll each ball individually in the desiccated coconut (optional).

6. Set balls onto the baking tray. Cover and chill in the fridge for 30 minutes to firm up.

Storage: Will keep in an airtight container in the fridge for up to five days, can be frozen for up to three months.

NO-BAKE FRUIT AND OAT BARS

Vegan • **Makes:** approximately 12 bars or 15 squares
Prep time: 15 minutes • **Chill time:** 3 hours

These healthy snack bars are a delicious alternative to shop-bought cereal bars. I created this recipe in order to make the most of my existing store-cupboard ingredients, and I encourage you to do the same. Using this recipe as a guide, switch up the nuts, dried fruit and seeds according to what you already have on hand – you can even add some dark chocolate pieces, if you like! Once the mix has set, you can cut it into small squares or larger slices, depending on your personal preference, then keep them in the fridge for when you're feeling peckish.

Benefits: Oats, nuts and dried fruit all help to contribute to the recommended 30g of fibre we should be aiming for each day. Nuts and dried fruit also provide iron.

Top tip: Choose darker chocolate for more antioxidants and plant-based goodness!

175g rolled oats
150g dried fruit (my favourite combination is 50g each of raisins, dried cranberries and dried apricots chopped into small pieces)
80g almonds, roughly chopped (or different nuts of your choice)
25g desiccated coconut
1 tbsp sesame seeds (or different seeds of your choice – you can use an extra tablespoon of chopped nuts if you prefer)
75g good-quality dark chocolate, at least 70% cocoa solids, chopped into small chunks (optional)
¼ tsp salt

½ tsp ground cinnamon
125g smooth almond butter
175g maple syrup

1. Line a 20×20cm (8×8 inch) square baking tin with non-stick baking paper, leaving some overhang for easy removal.

2. In a large, heat-proof bowl, mix together the oats, dried fruit, chopped nuts, desiccated coconut, sesame seeds, chopped dark chocolate (optional), salt and cinnamon. Set aside.

3. Place the almond butter and maple syrup in a small saucepan and set over a low–medium heat. Stir until melted, smooth and combined. Increase the heat to a simmer, stirring all the time. Gently simmer for about 30 seconds, stirring constantly, then remove from the heat.

4. Pour the melted nut butter/syrup mixture over the dry ingredients and mix well, until thoroughly combined.

5. Tip into the prepared baking tin and, using a spatula, firmly press it into an even layer – the more compact the mix is, the better the bars or squares will hold their shape.

6. Cover and chill in the fridge for at least 3 hours – or until completely firm all the way through.

7. Remove the mix from the tin and, using a sharp knife, cut into 12 equal-sized bars (or 15 smaller squares if desired). Enjoy!

Storage: Keep in an airtight container in the fridge for up to one week, can be frozen for up to three months.

WHAT ABOUT ULTRA-PROCESSED DRINKS?

Although this book is focused on ultra-processed foods (UPFs), we can't ignore drinks, because, let's face it, the line between snacks and drinks can be pretty blurred at times – is that mocha topped with whipped cream from the staff canteen at 10am a drink or a snack? Ultra-processed drinks (UPDs) are also very common in shops, and are often featured right next to the UPF snacks to drive consumption (clever marketing, hey!).

We are advised to drink around six to eight cups or glasses of fluid a day (200ml or 150ml cups or glasses respectively), however this is merely a guideline for the general population, and more fluid will be needed if it's hot or if you're particularly active, due to the loss of fluid through sweat. One of the easiest ways to tell if you're drinking enough is to look at the colour of your urine – if it's dark or concentrated, and you're not urinating often, then chances are you need to drink more. Aim for a urine colour that's near to pale straw, and don't forget that vitamin supplements can colour it bright yellow, so don't be alarmed at this (you're just looking at expensive wee!).

All fluids count towards our recommended fluid needs (at least 1.2 litres of fluid a day) – from soups to milk, water to smoothies, and teas and coffees too. In this part of the chapter, though, we are going to focus on 'traditional' drinks, and we will therefore class soup (however watery!) as a food (see Chapter 7: week 3 – lunches for more information). And although they can be calorific, we'll be including hot chocolate and squirty cream-topped mochas in this drinks section.

Are tea and coffee are dehydrating?

While caffeine has a slight diuretic (dehydrating) effect, especially when drunk in large quantities, there is almost always a net fluid gain, meaning that tea and coffee are classed as hydrating drinks. This is why it's a positive thing that in countries such as Italy, espressos (short coffees) are often served with a glass of water. A tip that I like to share is *remember to hydrate before you caffeinate* – this means getting into the habit of having a glass of water before your morning tea or coffee. This simple habit will help you to get in another glass of essential fluid for the day. It also helps to delay your morning coffee slightly, which can be beneficial for energy levels (experts recommend having your first morning dose of caffeine around an hour after waking).

Is caffeine bad for you?

As with everything, it is the portion size that determines whether food is healthy or unhealthy in the long term, and the same goes for caffeine. A general guideline for daily caffeine consumption is 300 to 400mg a day for adults; pregnant or breastfeeding women should keep to below 200mg a day. To put this number in context, one cup of instant coffee, or two cups of black tea (depending on the steeping time) contain about 100mg of caffeine. Coffee shop coffees can contain 400mg of caffeine or more per drink, so make sure to request just one shot, or decaf-feinated, if you're already nearing your suggested daily limit.

Pause to take a look at your food diary. How many cups or glasses of fluid have you drunk so far today? Have you had any water or has it been mainly teas, coffees, fizzy drinks and squash? There's nothing wrong with drinks other than water, but what we need to be mindful of is any UPDs or added sugar, which can easily add up over the course of a day. If you do decide to drink a UPD, do so purposefully and mindfully.

EXAMPLES OF NON-ULTRA-PROCESSED DRINKS VERSUS MORE- AND LESS-NUTRITIOUS ULTRA-PROCESSED DRINKS

Most UPDs contain sugars, as well as other additives, which can lead to excessive sugar and calorie consumption, as well as tooth decay. In addition, sugary drinks don't fill us up like food does, as there is minimal-to-zero fibre in them. For context, a 500ml bottle of cola contains over 12 teaspoons of sugar (over 50 grams), which is well over the entire 30g a day of free-sugar* intake recommended for adults. Children should be having no more than 19 to 24g of free-sugar* a day, depending on their age. So, although UPDs contain energy, they don't contain any other nutrients that contribute to health or wellbeing.

---

* As a reminder, free-sugar includes table sugar, sugar added to foods and drinks, and the sugars naturally occurring in fruit juice, honey and other syrups. It does not include the sugar found naturally in whole fruits or milk.

Non-UPD examples	More-nutritious or less energy-dense UPD examples	Less-nutritious or more energy-dense UPD examples
Water or milk (dairy)	Diet soda (this isn't more nutritious but it is lower in sugar)	Full-sugar sodas and energy drinks
100 per cent pure fruit juice (keep to 150ml maximum a day)	Kombucha or coconut water – choose no added sugar versions, ideally	Sweetened fruit juice drinks (juice drinks typically contain sugar and sweeteners)
Teas and coffees (with milk, no syrups)	Pre-made golden milk using fortified* almond milk	Golden-milk latte or hot chocolate from a chain coffee shop, with optional squirty cream
Sparkling water with fresh lemon or lime, or a handful of frozen berries	Sparkling water with lime flavouring – zero sugar (this isn't more nutritious but it is lower in sugar)	Sparkling water with full sugar syrup (lime or blackcurrant)

HOW TO CHOOSE BETWEEN TWO ULTRA-PROCESSED DRINKS

Let's look at the ingredients list and nutritional differences between two of the most common types of ultra-processed drinks: cola.

Branded cola in a can ingredients – *Carbonated Water, Sugar, Colour (Caramel E150d), Acid (Phosphoric Acid), Natural Flavourings including Caffeine.*

---

* Calcium and ideally iodine have been added

***Branded diet cola in a can ingredients** – Carbonated
Water, Colour (Caramel E150d), Sweeteners (Aspartame,
Acesulfame K), Natural Flavourings including Caffeine,
Acids (Phosphoric Acid, Citric Acid).*

The main difference between the two UPDs here is that the
diet cola contains artificial sweeteners rather than sugar. As
discussed in the introduction, artificial sweeteners have been
rigorously tested in the UK and worldwide, and are considered
safe for normal levels of consumption. Diet drinks are far from
being a health drink, though – just think of them as a less energy-
dense version of their full-sugar equivalents.

Water is, unsurprisingly, the ideal choice for helping you
to stay hydrated throughout the day without adding any
additional energy to your diet. UPDs can easily lead to
people consuming more energy than they need, so for most
people, UPDs are best consumed in moderation – I'm not
about to tell you to sip on a glass of water in the pub on a
Sunday afternoon, but you can if you want to!

TOP TIPS FOR HEALTHIER
NON-ULTRA-PROCESSED DRINKS

I could just tell you to drink more water, but instead have a look
at the following tips, pull out the ones that resonate with you,
then give them a go.

- **Buy yourself a nice reusable water bottle that you will
  enjoy drinking from:** this will save both money and plastic
  in the long term, and will help to keep you hydrated at the
  same time too.

- **Gradually reduce the sugar you add:** if you add sugar to your hot drinks, reduce it slowly so that your taste buds adapt over time. Try cutting the sugar by half a teaspoon per drink per day.

- **Choose no-added-sugar squash:** and try to drink less of it initially, before starting to make your drinks non-ultra-processed by adding natural flavours such as fresh mint leaves, slices of lemon or orange, or even sliced strawberries and cucumber.

- **Skip the coffee sachets:** for those who love their coffee, and lattes or cappuccinos in particular, try making them with just coffee and milk, as opposed to powdered sachets, which are ultra-processed.

- **Make balanced smoothies:** try to balance fruit with protein and vegetables for extra fibre – for example, balance berries and banana with yoghurt and a handful of spinach. I promise that adding a few spinach leaves will not change the taste of your smoothie, it will just colour it a little green.

- **Keep to 100 per cent fruit juice (can be from concentrate):** this is instead of 'juice drinks', which are UPDs. But limit your consumption of 100 per cent juice to 150ml a day maximum – you can add water or ice to make it go further.

What about alcohol?

The NHS recommends drinking no more than 14 units of alcohol a week, spread across three or more days. This is about six medium (175ml) glasses of wine, or six pints of four per cent beer. There's no completely safe level of drinking alcohol (other than not drinking it at all!), but keeping within these guidelines lowers your risk of harming your health. It may be interesting to know that NOVA classifies distilled alcoholic beverages such as whisky, gin, rum and vodka as 'ultra-processed', and fermented alcoholic beverages such as beer, alcoholic cider and wine as 'processed' – neither is better for you from a health point of view, however the ultra-processed alcoholic drinks are designed to be drunk in smaller quantities due to their much higher percentage ABV (alcohol by volume).

HEALTHY NON-UPD IDEAS

The following drinks are not ultra-processed, and are naturally low in calories and sugar too. Which do you prefer?

- Plain water – filtered, tap or sparkling

- Water with fruit, e.g. lemon, orange or strawberries – in summer these fruits can be frozen into ice cubes for a cooling and refreshing drink

- Hot or cold water with herbs such as mint leaves

- Herbal teas, e.g. peppermint, chamomile or fruit tea (see page 107 for my recipe for Lemon, ginger and honey tea)

- Black tea or coffee with or without milk (no added sugar or sweetener).

HOW TO ORGANISE YOUR KITCHEN FOR HEALTHIER DRINKING

Healthier living starts with your environment – have a look in your kitchen and make sure that it's set up for success this week.

- Keep a jug or bottle of chilled water, with slices of fruit if desired, in the fridge so it's more appealing to drink. Change the water and fruits daily.

- Freeze water to make ice cubes if you prefer cold water. Slices of lemon can be added before freezing for a natural flavour.

- Stock your cupboards with various herbal teas for flavourful drinks without added sugar or caffeine.

- Keep sodas and fizzy drinks out of the fridge (if unopened) so that they are less appealing to drink mid-week.

MEAL PLANNER WITH NON-UPF SNACKS AND DRINKS

Now that you have got a grip on snacks, we can move on to thinking about drinks. By planning ahead, you can make more exciting and healthier choices when it comes to drinks. Aim for the majority of your fluids (at least 1.2 litres a day) to be water (and sugar-free tea and coffee, remembering to keep your caffeine intake to within appropriate limits and ideally before mid-afternoon so it doesn't impact your sleep!), but if you fancy something a little different, check out the following suggestions, too.

	Monday	Tuesday	Wednesday	
Breakfast				
Morning snack	Apple and cheese	Oatcakes topped with nut butter and banana slices	Berries with plain yoghurt and a drizzle of honey if desired	
Lunch				
Afternoon snack	Carrots and hummus – homemade (see recipe on page 85) or shop bought	Dark chocolate and coconut energy balls (see recipe on page 88)	Small bag of popcorn – or pop at home with kernels	
Evening meal				
Dessert/ evening snack				
Drinks	Water and warm golden milk with turmeric	Water and hot chocolate made from warm milk, cocoa powder and a dash of maple syrup	Water and strawberry- and cucumber- infused water	

Week 1 – snacks and drinks

	Thursday	Friday	Saturday	Sunday
	Healthy trail mix – made from plain nuts, dried fruit and dark chocolate	Dried apricots and almonds	Medjool dates stuffed with nut butter and a little dark chocolate	Avocado on a wholegrain cracker with slices of boiled egg
	Roasted butter beans with olive oil and spices	No-bake fruit and oat bars (see recipe on page 90)	Pear and a handful of walnuts	Roasted kale crisps
	Water and herbal tea of choice	Water and lemon, ginger and honey tea (see recipe on page 107)	Water and fresh carrot and orange juice (see recipe on page 105)	Water and date, banana and cocoa smoothie (see recipe on page 104)

YOUR FIVE-STEP HEALTHY CHECKLIST
FOR WEEK 1 (DRINKS)

Have a look at your food diary so far – how often are ultra-processed drinks creeping in?

In the following table are some examples of goals you could focus on for the week and month ahead. Using the information from your food diary, think about which of these goals resonate with you, or which you'd find easy to do, and start with those (or come up with your own goals).

Tick on the left if you want to work on a particular goal, and on the right when you have achieved it:

Tick to work on ✔	Goal	Tick when completed ✔
	Replace sugary drinks with diet drinks (step one), herbal teas, or better yet, water (step two) to be non-ultra-processed.	
	Stop putting sugar in tea and coffee – gradually reduce it if you struggle to do this at first.	
	Stick to decaffeinated tea and coffee after 2 or 3pm to support your sleep hygiene (sleep is crucial for making better choices the following day).	
	Drink a glass of water before your first drink of the day (unless your first drink is already water!).	
	Experiment with herb-, fruit- and vegetable-infused water to increase consumption.	

NON-UPD HEALTHY DRINK RECIPES

If you're keen to try something a little different, or just want to reduce your caffeine, sugar or alcohol intake, have a go at any of the three following recipes, before reflecting on this week's challenges and changes.

- Date, banana and cocoa smoothie

- Fresh carrot and orange juice

- Lemon, ginger and honey tea

DATE, BANANA AND COCOA SMOOTHIE

Vegetarian/adaptable for vegans • Makes: 1 glass
Prep time: 5 minutes

This homemade smoothie has a wonderful chocolate flavour thanks to the cocoa powder, and a deliciously creamy texture. It is perfect as an on-the-go breakfast, a substantial snack, or poured into lolly moulds and frozen for a healthier homemade ice lolly. You can swap the Greek yoghurt for kefir for extra probiotics or, if you follow a vegan diet, opt for a fortified plant-based yoghurt (and milk) instead.

Benefits: Greek yoghurt is rich in protein in addition to calcium, which is needed for healthy bones. Kefir is a fermented food which contains live bacteria and contributes to good gut health. We should all try to include fermented foods in our diet on a regular basis.

½ frozen banana – use a ripe medium banana and peel before freezing (in a freezer bag)
3 medjool dates, pitted
1–2 tsp of cocoa powder
200ml milk of choice
2 tbsp of Greek yoghurt, kefir or plant-based option

1. Place all of the ingredients into a blender and blitz until smooth and creamy.

2. Pour into a glass and enjoy.

Storage: This drink is best enjoyed immediately, but can be covered and kept in the fridge for 24 hours. Alternatively, pour into lolly moulds and freeze for up to three months.

FRESH CARROT AND ORANGE JUICE

Vegetarian/adaptable for vegans • **Makes:** 2 glasses
Prep time: 5 minutes

There has been lots of controversy about shop-bought fruit juice drinks and, while I always believe in everything in moderation, making your own freshly squeezed version of orange juice allows you to know exactly what you're drinking. Although it might sound odd, I add carrot to mine – the flavour works really well, and it is a good way to add extra nutrients. You can also pour the mixture into ice lolly moulds and freeze for a refreshing chilled treat on a hot summer's day. You can make this drink vegan-friendly by swapping the honey for a sweetener that is suitable for vegans, such as maple syrup.

Benefits: This freshly squeezed juice is a good source of vitamin C, which helps support a healthy immune system. Vitamin C also aids the absorption of plant-based iron, so ideally enjoy this juice alongside an iron-rich meal.

2 large oranges, zested and peeled
1 medium-sized carrot, peeled and chopped
250–300ml water
1–2 tsp honey or maple syrup (optional)

1. Add the orange zest, peeled oranges, carrot, 250ml water and your chosen sweetener (if using) to a blender and blitz until smooth and combined. Check the consistency and add more liquid, if needed.

2. Taste and add more honey or maple syrup, to taste, if desired.

3. Blend again to combine before pouring into glasses and enjoying.

Storage: This drink is best enjoyed immediately, but can be covered and kept in the fridge for 24 hours. Alternatively, pour into lolly moulds and freeze for up to three months.

LEMON, GINGER AND HONEY TEA

Vegetarian/adaptable for vegans • **Makes:** 2 teacups
Prep time: 10 minutes

There is nothing more comforting than a warming cup of tea on a cold morning (or evening!) – and this lemon, ginger and honey recipe is one of my favourites. It is so simple to make and is ideal if you are looking for a delicious, caffeine-free way to stay hydrated.

Benefits: Lemon is a good source of vitamin C, which helps support the immune system, while the caffeine-free nature of the drink means that it will not disrupt sleep.

1 unwaxed lemon – zest and juice (about 2–3 tbsp)
3cm piece of root ginger, grated
500ml boiling water
1–2 tbsp honey or maple syrup, to taste

To serve
Slices of lemon (optional)

1. Add the lemon zest, juice and grated ginger to a teapot. Pour in the boiling water and add 1 tablespoon of honey or maple syrup. Stir gently and leave to infuse for 10 minutes.

2. Taste, and adjust the sweetness if desired.

3. Place a small mesh strainer over your cup and pour the tea through.

4. Add a slice of lemon to the cup (optional) and serve.

Storage: This tea is best enjoyed immediately after making, but can be cooled completely, covered and kept in the fridge for up to three days. When ready to reheat, do so in a saucepan over medium heat, then pour into cups.

END OF WEEK 1 (SNACKS AND DRINKS) REFLECTION

How did you find your first week? Manageable? Challenging? With anything new, it is important to monitor progress and reflect on what was done well (i.e. the new healthy habits that have been formed) and what you would still like to work on. What does success in week 1 look like to you?

Reflections should go beyond simply reviewing your food choices and should extend to your motivations and your overall wellbeing. If you feel like you have made progress, be sure to celebrate the small wins.

Reflection questions

Answer these in your mind or put pen to paper (the latter is almost always more beneficial when it comes to making changes):

- **How have your snack and drink choices gone so far this week?** Think back on what food and drink options were available to you and what was eaten and drunk – have there been any shifts towards more unprocessed or minimally processed snacks and drinks since reading this book? Or are you now having more of the more-nutritious ultra-processed snacks and fewer of the less-nutritious ultra-processed drinks?

- **What small wins should we celebrate?** Identify specific instances in which you made healthier decisions, resisted temptation, or discovered delicious healthier snack or drink options. For example, perhaps you went with fruit and yoghurt for a mid-morning snack instead of a croissant with jam. What made these achievements possible?

- **What obstacles did you encounter?** Pinpoint any moments where it became difficult for you to meet your goals, such as triggers, lack of preparation, emotional states or social situations. Understanding any barriers and what you found hard is important. Perhaps it was the free toast and jam at work that you found hard to resist, or the fish and chips with an alcoholic drink after work. Brainstorm a list of possible solutions – this is known as solution-focused problem solving and will be very specific to you and your situation.

- **How have your choices affected both your physical and mental wellbeing?** Consider any noticeable shifts in energy levels, mood, digestion and sleep quality over the past week. Can you attribute any of those to your dietary changes?

- **What patterns or habits have you observed recently?** Do specific times, emotions or environments influence your food and beverage selections? Recognising these trends will bring about awareness so you can make different changes in the future.

Based on your reflections, what areas need improvement over the next week? Identify one or two goals – these could include meal planning, setting aside time for food shopping, trying new recipes or finding healthier ways to cope with stress or boredom that do not involve UPFs, UPDs or alcohol.

Now you know the areas that you want to work on regarding your snacks and drinks, what is the first action you want to take? Make a note of it in your food diary and work on it over the following week while we take a look at your breakfast options. It's time to head into week 2.

CHAPTER 6

WEEK 2 – BREAKFASTS

Welcome to week 2! Now we're going to focus on breakfast, the first meal of the day. Breakfast can be a great way to set the tone of the day as it is the first thing we eat after waking. Having a high-protein, nutrient-packed breakfast has the power to keep you feeling full until lunchtime, as well as getting you off to a flying start in terms of meeting your fruit, vegetable and fibre goals for the day. However, it's also a meal that can easily centre around UPFs – from sugary cereals to processed pastries, highly processed yoghurts to poor-quality breads. This week, we will explore how to make breakfast a UPF-free zone – or at least a significantly reduced UPF zone – for the majority of the time.

What about intermittent fasting (IF)?

Intermittent fasting (IF) is a dieting technique where there are periods of time when you don't eat, and in some cases, periods of time when you don't drink either. Most fasts though, including the popular 16:8 fast (where you only consume food during an eight-hour window each day), do allow for water as well as black tea and coffee outside of the eating window. I often get asked about IF and whether I would recommend it. My answer is that it truly depends on individual factors such as activity level, lifestyle and hunger level, as well as other medical conditions, such as diabetes, and associated medications. It is for this reason that IF isn't recommended for everyone – in particular, it is not recommended to those prone to low blood sugar levels, disordered eating or eating disorders, children, pregnant people and those who breastfeed.

Sometimes individuals do fast naturally without even realising it; for example, someone may eat their evening meal early, then wake up the next day and not feel hungry until 11am. Keep in mind, though, that concentration and energy levels may be affected due to long gaps between meals, and you don't want to leave it too long, as your food choices may be affected (many people miss subtle signs of hunger, and we want to avoid feelings of ravenousness!).

While fasting may have some health benefits according to emerging research, the evidence base for this is still fairly new, and it's essential to make any eating plan work for you. One place I often start at with my patients is to try a 10- to 12-hour fast overnight. This might mean eating your last meal by 7pm and not having breakfast until 7am. Your gut likes to have a break, and overnight isn't a time for heavy meals or UPFs.

Regardless of when you have breakfast, the primary aim is to consume a meal that has a balance of nutrients, particularly focused on fruits or vegetables, wholegrains and protein. One of the reasons why you might crave a mid-morning ultra-processed snack is because your breakfast could be lacking in fibre or protein. Including these components will mean better digestive health, balanced blood sugar levels and more satisfaction too.

NON-UPF VERSUS UPF-BREAKFAST OPTIONS

There's often a big difference between a non-UPF and a UPF breakfast nutritionally. A non-UPF breakfast typically consists of whole, minimally processed foods that provide a balanced mix of macronutrients (proteins, fats and carbohydrates with fibre) and essential vitamins and minerals. For example, a bowl of porridge made with milk, and topped with sliced banana, crushed walnuts and cinnamon. On the other hand, UPF breakfasts (chocolate- and honey-coated cereals as well as chocolate pastries, to name just a few popular choices) often rely heavily on added sugars, unhealthy fats and refined grains, offering less fibre and failing to keep you satisfied throughout the morning. As I've said before though, there can be space in a healthy and balanced diet for these types of foods, but choosing non-UPF breakfasts the majority of the time will help to ensure you're having a delicious and healthy start to your day.

Thankfully, there are many non-ultra-processed convenient breakfast options available in the supermarkets – from porridge oats (if you have more time), to wheat biscuits, both of which are a step towards a more nutritious and satiating breakfast. Even though some higher-fibre and lower-sugar options may be processed to some degree, not all processing is bad, and it's the ingredients list that matters when it comes to monitoring our UPF intake – look for breakfast cereals that are free from additives such as preservatives, artificial colours or flavours and emulsifiers (I am not referring to added vitamins and minerals here which are beneficial to health, instead I am referring to ingredients not commonly found in the home kitchen).

As illustrated in the table that follows, porridge or wheat biscuits are an ideal convenient non-processed breakfast option that I would recommend. Oats are high in fibre and help optimise cholesterol levels while also contributing to the daily 30g of fibre goal. They are also naturally low in sugar and can be sweetened in a non-UPF manner with fruit or even a little pure maple syrup. Oats also act as a good base for adding in protein such as a nut butter or Greek yoghurt, to boost fullness levels even further.

Did you know that oats have a relatively low glycaemic index (GI)?

The GI is a scale, from 0–100, that indicates the speed at which the carbohydrates we eat are broken down into glucose, and how much of a rise in blood glucose (sugar) levels this can cause. High-GI foods release their energy (glucose/sugar) into the bloodstream relatively quickly, whereas low-GI foods release their energy relatively slowly, which means more sustained energy. A low-GI diet is often recommended for health, and involves:

- swapping high-GI foods for low-GI alternatives where possible, e.g. corn flakes for porridge oats

- consuming high-GI foods with low-GI foods or protein/ fat to lower the overall GI of the meal/snack, e.g. a jacket potato with tuna and salad

- basing meals around plant-based (typically low-GI) foods such as wholegrains, fruits and vegetables, alongside protein and healthy fats too.

Some examples of lower-GI carbohydrates typically eaten at breakfast time include porridge oats, most fruits and sourdough or seeded breads. Remember though, it's OK to have higher-GI foods, e.g. corn flakes or regular white bread, especially when combined with protein, fat and fibre such as milk, nut butter, fruit or even eggs.

Non-UPF breakfast examples	More-nutritious or less energy-dense UPF breakfast examples	Less-nutritious or more energy-dense UPF breakfast examples
Overnight oats or porridge with milk and Greek yoghurt, topped with nuts and berries	Multigrain hoop cereal or corn flakes with milk	Chocolate- or honey-coated cereal with milk
Wheat biscuits with semi-skimmed milk	High-fibre wheat squares with milk	Sugar-frosted wheat squares with milk
Greek yoghurt with homemade granola, fruit, seeds and a little honey	Low-sugar fruit yoghurt with shop-bought granola and berries	Chocolate or fruit corner-style yoghurt (high in added sugar)
Sourdough bread (traditionally made) with nut butter and sliced banana	Wholemeal toast with an olive oil-based spread and baked beans	Long-life chocolate croissants or pastries

Baked beans are technically a UPF but they are more nutritious than most, given that they provide an abundance of protein and fibre too. Most of the sugar on the nutrition label is naturally occurring from the tomatoes, and just three tablespoons of baked beans counts as one of your five a day, so they are not a food to be avoided in my professional opinion. Baked beans are a clear example of why, although it can be useful to think about where we are consuming UPFs within our diet, the designation of a product as a UPF can't be used in isolation to determine whether or not a food is 'healthy'.

HOW TO CHOOSE THE BEST BREAKFAST

Let's look at the nutritional difference between two of the cereal choices that were listed in the breakfast examples table.

UPF frosted wheat breakfast cereal ingredients – *Wholewheat (84%), Sugar, Humectant (Sorbitol), Beef Gelatin*

Non-UPF wheat biscuit ingredients – *Wholegrain Wheat (100%)*

The UPF cereal is primarily made of wholewheat, which is positive, but it's coated with sugar and includes sorbitol (a sugar alcohol used as a sweetener, and humectant to retain moisture) and beef gelatin (used as a binder or to add texture). A 40g portion contains 6.8g of sugar, however the reality is that the average portion of cereal that people serve themselves could be double this. In contrast, the non-UPF cereal contains just 0.3g of sugar per 45g portion and is made entirely from wholegrain wheat. This would be an easy swap to help immediately reduce the number of UPFs in your diet.

'Food fortification' is defined as the practice of adding nutrients to foods, including vitamins and minerals, in order to increase their nutritional value. If you need to optimise your iron levels, choose 'fortified' cereals, i.e. those that have added iron in them. Iron helps transport oxygen around the body, which is why if you are deficient, you'll feel tired. This can be especially common among women. Iron is also found in red meat (haem-iron found in red meat is relatively easy for the body to absorb), leafy greens, nuts, dried fruit such as apricots, and beans such as red kidney beans. However, it's essential to read labels carefully; not all fortified foods are created the same. Some may also be high in added sugars or unhealthy fats. Choosing products that offer a balance of nutrients without excessive additives, such as emulsifiers, is the aim. If you don't like cereals, adding spinach to your omelette or smoothie is one simple way of increasing iron consumption. Pairing iron-rich plant-foods with a source of vitamin C, like an orange or tomatoes, increases the absorption of iron, while drinking tea and coffee can inhibit absorption. If you are deficient in iron, make sure to leave a 60-minute gap between eating your fortified cereal and drinking your morning brew (hard, I know!).

Let's also compare two UPF versions and one non-UPF version of another very popular breakfast item: yoghurt.

Less-nutritious UPF chocolate balls with yoghurt ingredients – *Yoghurt (**Milk**), Sugar, Water, Cocoa Butter, **Milk** Powder, Rice Flour, Wholemeal **Wheat** Flour (Gluten), **Wheat** Flour (with added Calcium, Iron, Niacin, Thiamin), Cocoa Mass, Modified Starch, **Wheat** Fibre, **Wheat** Bran, Glucose Syrup, Coconut Oil, Flavourings, Colour: Carotenes; Lactose (**Milk**), Glazing Agent: Acacia Gum; Sweet Whey*

Powder (**Milk**), **Barley** Malt, **Barley** Flour, Salt, **Milk** Protein, Stabiliser: Pectins; Emulsifier: **Soya** Lecithin.

More-nutritious UPF fruit-flavoured yoghurt pot ingredients – Yogurt (**Milk**), Kiwi (8%), Sugar, Modified Maize Starch, Natural Flavouring, Stabiliser (Pectin), **Milk** Minerals + Live Cultures (Lactobacillus Bulgaricus, Streptococcus Thermophilus, Lactococcus Lactis, Bifidobacterium Lactis).

Non-UPF plain Greek yoghurt ingredients – Natural Greek Yoghurt (**Milk**), Live Cultures [S. Thermophilus, L. Bulgaricus]

One pot of the less-nutritious UPF yoghurt contains 21g of sugar (this includes the sugar from the milk as well as any added sugar), which is a relatively high amount when compared with a plain yoghurt. The ingredients list is also long and includes flavourings, colours, flour types, modified starch and emulsifiers, making this a clear UPF. I suggest treating yoghurts such as these as more of a dessert option, rather than a healthy start to the day.

The second UPF option is a healthier alternative, as it contains significantly lower levels of sugar (just 14g per pot). Plus, it contains a higher percentage of natural ingredients such as kiwi fruit. Furthermore, the yoghurt itself is made from milk with live cultures, and the added kiwi adds flavour without the need for an excess in free-sugar – providing you with all of the bene-fits associated with live active cultures (aka probiotics for gut health), with only moderate levels of added sweetness.

For optimal gut health, nothing beats natural Greek yoghurt containing milk and live cultures – offering only nutrient-dense ingredients with probiotic benefits. At under 4g of natural sugar per similar-size serving, it has the lowest sugar content of all the yoghurts in this example. Adding your own fruit for sweetness adds extra fibre and vitamins, without contributing to your daily free-sugar intake.

What are probiotics?

These are live bacteria that can help diversify the gut microbiome. Think of your gut like a garden; the more diverse the range of flowers and plants you have, the better the ecosystem is. You may like to know that more than 90 per cent of the happy hormone serotonin is made in your gut, and around 70 per cent of your immune cells are there too, so what you eat really can influence your mind, and helps protect you from illnesses too.

I'm often asked if probiotic supplements are useful to take – my answer, as always, is that it depends on the situation, however there is research to show that they can be beneficial if someone is taking, or has been taking, antibiotics.

Now, let's turn our attention to bread. Not just a staple of breakfasts across the country every morning, but also a staple of our lunches.

Less-nutritious UPF supermarket loaf, WHITE LOAF ingredients – Wheat Flour (with added Calcium, Iron, Niacin, Thiamin), Water, Yeast, Salt, Soya Flour, Preservative: E282, Emulsifiers: E472e, E471, E481, Rapeseed Oil, Flour Treatment Agent: Ascorbic Acid.

More-nutritious UPF supermarket loaf, SOURFAUX* (says 'contains sourdough' on the label) ingredients – Wheat

---

* 'Sourfaux breads' are breads named or marketed using the word sourdough, despite not being manufactured using traditional methods that use minimal added ingredients. True sourdough bread is naturally leavened, which means it doesn't use commercial yeast to make it rise.

*Flour [**Wheat** Flour, Calcium Carbonate, Iron, Niacin, Thiamin], Water, Yeast, Salt, **Wheat** Bran, Preservative (Calcium Propionate), Emulsifiers (Mono- and Di-Glycerides of Fatty Acids, Mono- and Di-Acetyl Tartaric Acid Esters of Mono- and Di-Glycerides of Fatty Acids), Spirit Vinegar, Flour Treatment Agent (Ascorbic Acid).*

***Non-UPF supermarket loaf, SOURDOUGH ingredients –** Wheat Flour (**Wheat** Flour, Calcium Carbonate, Iron, Niacin, Thiamin), Water, **Rye** Flour, Salt, Fermented **Wheat** Flour.*

The above examples show how a similar type of bread (white, sliced) from the supermarket can vary from a non-UPF (sourdough), to a more-nutritious UPF (sourfaux), to a less-than-nutritious UPF (simple white loaf). Finances may play a role in which bread you choose to buy on a regular basis, and so if you do buy the UPF varieties, just remember to choose wholemeal wherever possible, and that quantity matters, in addition to your chosen toppings – think avocado and eggs versus a chocolate spread!

THE IMPACT OF UPF BREAKFAST CHOICES ON YOUR DAILY WELLBEING

We can all relate to how food impacts our mood and mental clarity. When we eat nutritious foods, we feel good and have better concentration for tasks. Starting the day as we mean to go on is a good mindset to have, and this is why many people choose to exercise in the morning – that, and the fact that it's great to get your workout out of the way early. Choosing a healthy breakfast sends a signal to your mind that you're taking time to nourish yourself, and I'm sure your gut will thank you for it too!

TOP TIPS FOR A HEALTHIER, LESS-PROCESSED BREAKFAST

As with anything, preparation is key, so putting some thought behind how you can include more whole foods in your morning routine will be well worth it. Have a look at the following tips to see which you could apply to your morning meal.

- **Read food labels:** when it comes to breakfast cereals, breads and yoghurts, compare the ingredients lists. Typically, the shorter the list, the better; look for fewer additives (with the exception of added vitamins) and less added sugar.

- **Incorporate fruit:** improve your breakfast with a portion of fresh, frozen or dried fruit. When it comes to serving sizes, use a small, cupped hand for dried fruit, an open hand for fresh fruit and around 3 tablespoons for frozen. Adding fruit helps to increase fibre intake and provides essential vitamins without any added free-sugar. I personally love berries or stewed apples with cinnamon as a breakfast topper.

- **Swap to wholegrain:** choosing a wholemeal bread or cereal over white refined carbohydrates is a simple way to instantly boost your fibre and satiety levels while also improving gut health.

- **Sprinkle some seeds:** an easy way to boost fibre intake, healthy fats and plant-based diversity at breakfast time is to sprinkle some seeds over whatever you're eating. My go-to is chia and flaxseeds for their omega-3 content, as well as pumpkin and sunflower seeds. These healthy fats benefit our hearts and promote healthy cholesterol levels. If you're not a fan of seeds, add some ground or flaked nuts – walnuts and almonds work well at breakfast time on both cereal and toast.

- **Experiment with new ingredients:** if you always have cereal, why not try an egg-based dish high in vitamin B12, vitamin D and protein with tomatoes and spinach? Or if you're vegan, swap this for scrambled tofu sprinkled with fortified nutritional yeast.

- **Choose natural sweeteners in moderation:** if you need to sweeten your breakfast, opt for natural sweeteners such as a little honey or pure maple syrup, mashed banana or grated apple, instead of refined sugars or artificial sweeteners. Remember, moderation is key, as even natural sweeteners such as honey and maple syrup contain free-sugars and are not any healthier than refined sugar, as the body still processes them in the same way. If you do want a non-sugar sweetener, go for stevia or xylitol, which are plant-based.

- **Look for fortified plant-based milks:** if you opt for plant-based milk over dairy, make sure on the back of the carton it says that it has added calcium and ideally iodine too (especially if you don't consume white fish), so you don't risk nutrient deficiency and poor bone health. For added protein, choose soya milk over nut- or oat-based milks.

- **Batch prep:** overnight oats, baked oats, egg-based muffins and homemade breakfast bars all last a few days in the fridge, and so are good for when you don't have time to prep anything in the morning.

- **Incorporate proteins and fibre:** the reason why you might be feeling hungry mid-morning is the fact you are missing protein (found in eggs, milk, yoghurt and nuts) and fibre (found in fruits, vegetables and wholegrains). Make sure that your breakfast contains both of these components.

- **Make green smoothies:** if you're a fan of smoothies, add some vegetables and protein to balance out the natural sugars from fruit. For example, combine leafy greens (like spinach or kale) with a banana or berries for sweetness, then add a base of Greek yoghurt or plant-based milk. For added protein, consider including a scoop of nut butter or a spoonful of hemp seeds. For speed, you can even make up 'smoothie bags' containing fruit and greens and keep them in the freezer. When you want to make a smoothie, simply put the bag of frozen produce, along with any milk or yoghurt, into your blender, and whizz it all up.

HEALTHY NON-UPF BREAKFAST IDEAS

Here are ten of my favourite non-UPF ways to start the day – there's a variety of both sweet and savoury options so that all taste preferences are accounted for! Check out the recipes at the end of this chapter for more inspiration, and remember, breakfast doesn't need to be different every single day of the week, you could alternate between your favourite two or three.

1 **Overnight oats:** make with equal parts oats, milk and yoghurt, then top with fruit and nuts for the following day.

2 **Porridge:** this can be made on the hob or in the microwave, and can then be topped with fruit, seeds, cinnamon and a little honey for sweetness if desired.

3 **Avocado and scrambled eggs or scrambled tofu on non-UPF wholemeal or seeded toast:** top with tomatoes and spinach for a filling breakfast.

4 **Sourdough toast topped with pesto, pan-fried halloumi and mushrooms:** adding a side of wilted spinach is optional for even more plant diversity.

5 **Homemade granola or muesli:** serve with your preferred milk and fruit.

6 **100 per cent wheat biscuits:** top with milk, fruit and flaked almonds.

7 **Baked eggs (shakshuka):** I serve mine with sourdough toast.

8 **Smoothie:** make your own with fruit, milk, yoghurt and spinach. One of my favourite bases for a smoothie is using half a frozen banana (peel first before freezing!), a handful of berries, a cup of milk, a spoon of yoghurt if I have it in, and spinach too.

9 **Homemade breakfast bar or baked oats:** both of these options can contain oats, fruit and nuts.

10 **Your own full English:** my favourite healthy version is scrambled eggs with grilled tomatoes, homemade baked beans, mushrooms and sourdough toast.

SHOPPING LIST EASY WINS – YOUR KITCHEN ESSENTIALS

Some of these items may already be in your kitchen from week 1, and if so, they can be ticked off straight away.

Fresh produce and fridge items

- **Bananas, berries or kiwi**

- **Avocados**

- **Variety of breakfast-friendly vegetables** like tomatoes, mushrooms and spinach.

- **Eggs or plain (calcium-set) tofu**

- **Dairy or plant-based milk**, ideally fortified with calcium.

- **Plain yoghurt**

Cupboard items

- **Plain oats** for porridge

- **Wheat biscuits**

- **Sourdough or non-UPF wholemeal bread**

- **Nuts**, such as almonds, walnuts, Brazil nuts, cashews or mixed nuts (plain).

- **Seeds**, such as sunflower, pumpkin, sesame or chia (plain).

- **Nut butters** (peanut, almond or cashew).

- **Tinned fruit**, in juice not syrup.

Frozen foods

- **Frozen fruits**, such as mixed berries, mango and banana for smoothies.

HOW TO ORGANISE YOUR KITCHEN FOR BREAKFAST SUCCESS

Healthy habits and food choices are made easier when our environment nudges us towards better options. You may have made some of the following changes already, but if not, make them now in week 2.

- Organise your breakfast cereals so oats and no-added-sugar cereals are in front of any sugar-coated varieties. For bonus points, decant your oats into a large glass mason jar or container and pop in a cup measurer for easy scooping on a morning (use a heaped half cup per portion).

- Keep your fruit bowl stocked with fresh fruit that you enjoy eating.

- Organise your cupboards into different sections – separate carbs, such as breads and oats, from proteins, such as beans, and tinned or dried fruit, so you can find things easily.

- Keep a supply of frozen fruits in your freezer for overnight oats, porridge toppings, homemade chia seed jam and smoothies, too.

- Dedicate a section of your fridge to breakfast items, such as yoghurt and berries.

- Keep your blender out so it is easy to access.

MEAL PLANNER WITH NON-UPF SNACKS, DRINKS AND BREAKFASTS

Taking the time to plan which breakfast you will have each day means that your brain doesn't have to do much in the way of thinking come the morning, and instead you can just grab or make, eat and go! The examples here are suggestions, but in reality, you may alternate between just two or three healthy breakfast choices across a week.

	Monday	Tuesday	Wednesday
Breakfast	Overnight oats (see recipe on page 136) with nut butter and banana	Butterbean shakshuka (see recipe on page 141)	Vegan oaty blueberry muffins (see recipe on page 134)
Morning snack	Apple and cheese	Oatcakes topped with nut butter and banana slices	Berries with plain yoghurt and a drizzle of honey if desired
Lunch			
Afternoon snack	Carrots and hummus – homemade (see recipe on page 85) or shop bought	Dark chocolate and coconut energy balls (see recipe on page 88)	Small bag of popcorn – or pop at home with kernels
Evening meal			
Dessert/ evening snack			
Drinks	Water and warm golden milk with turmeric	Water and hot chocolate made from warm milk, cocoa powder and a dash of maple syrup	Water and strawberry- and cucumber infused-water

Thursday	Friday	Saturday	Sunday
Peanut butter and banana on wholegrain toast	Greek yoghurt pancakes (see recipe on page 132)	Sweet potato fritters (see recipe on page 139)	Spinach and mushroom omelette
Healthy trail mix – made from plain nuts, dried fruit and dark chocolate	Dried apricots and almonds	Medjool dates stuffed with nut butter and a little dark chocolate	Avocado on a wholegrain cracker with slices of boiled egg
Roasted butter beans with olive oil and spices	No-bake fruit and oat bars (see recipe on page 90)	Pear and a handful of walnuts	Roasted kale crisps
Water and herbal tea of choice	Water and lemon, ginger and honey tea (see recipe on page 107)	Water and fresh carrot and orange juice (see recipe on page 105)	Water and date, banana and cocoa smoothie (see recipe on page 104)

YOUR FIVE-STEP HEALTHY CHECKLIST FOR WEEK 2 (BREAKFAST)

As we started last week, take a look at the example goals in the following table and choose which you want to work on over the next week and beyond. You can also come up with your own goals.

Tick on the left if you want to work on a particular goal, and on the right when you have achieved it:

Tick to work on ✔	Goal	Tick when completed ✔
	Make sure your cupboards contain non-UPF carbohydrates such as oats, 100 per cent wheat biscuits and sourdough or wholemeal bread.	
	Start your day hydrating with a glass of water or herbal tea.	
	Add one handful of fruit or veg to your breakfast every day, e.g. add fruit to porridge or tomatoes to eggs.	
	If you like yoghurt, make sure your fridge includes (non-UPF) plain yoghurt.	
	Make a mixed seed or nut jar as a breakfast topper. Dried fruit can also be added.	

NON-UPF HEALTHY BREAKFAST RECIPES

Breakfast doesn't need to be different every day of the week, but you may want to try one or two of the following five recipes each week, to help you to reduce your reliance on UPFs in the morning.

- Greek yoghurt pancakes

- Vegan oaty blueberry muffins

- Overnight oats – four ways

- Sweet potato fritters

- Butterbean shakshuka

GREEK YOGHURT PANCAKES

Vegetarian • **Serves:** 1 to 2 people
Prep time: 10 minutes • **Cook time:** 10 minutes

This pancake recipe first appeared on my blog in 2012, and is my go-to recipe when I want something quick, simple and nourishing. As well as changing the flavour of the pancakes themselves by adding cinnamon or vanilla, I also love experimenting with different flours and toppings, such as homemade fruit compote, seasonal berries, sliced banana, nut butter or chopped nuts – all of which can help pack in extra nutrients.

Benefits: Greek yoghurt is a good source of protein and calcium – as well as probiotics to help support gut health.

For the pancakes
2 eggs
40g oat flour,* buckwheat flour, plain, or self-raising flour
1 tsp baking powder, for extra fluffiness (omit if using self-raising flour)
100g Greek yoghurt

For the flavours
1–2 tsp of ground cinnamon, honey or vanilla extract
Vegetable (rapeseed) oil, for cooking

To serve
Your choice of toppings – for example, berries, sliced banana, homemade fruit compote, nut butter, honey, maple syrup and/or melted dark chocolate

---

* oat flour can be made by simply blending oats until milled

1. Add the eggs, flour, baking powder (if using), Greek yoghurt and flavour of your choice to a medium-sized bowl.

2. Whisk until light, fluffy and combined.

3. Set a large frying pan over a medium heat, then add a splash of oil and swirl round the pan. Drop heaped spoonfuls of the batter into the pan to create small pancakes – taking care to leave enough space for the pancakes to expand (start by cooking one at a time).

4. Cook for 1–2 minutes, until the bottom is set and easily comes away from the pan, before using a spatula to flip the pancake, then cooking for a further 1–2 minutes until the pancake is completely cooked through. Remove from the pan and place onto a plate. Repeat with the remaining batter until all has been used up.

5. Stack the pancakes onto serving plates and top with your favourite toppings.

Storage: Best served warm straight away, or extra pancakes can be stored for up to five days in the fridge in an airtight container. Warm for 15–30 seconds on a heat-safe plate in the microwave. Alternatively, freeze the pancakes between layers of non-stick baking paper (or in a single layer) in a freezer bag.

VEGAN OATY BLUEBERRY MUFFINS

Vegan • **Makes:** 12 servings • **Prep time:** 10 minutes
Bake time: 20–25 minutes

Blueberry muffins are a hugely popular breakfast/snack option – but many shop-bought versions can be very high in sugar and rely on UPFs for their taste and texture. That is why I created my healthier homemade version with added oats for fibre, and vanilla for sweetness. I always make sure I have a batch in the freezer ready for when I need a quick breakfast or want to offer friends and family something when they come round for a catch up. Just a note on the blueberries: while you could use frozen blueberries, they can make the muffins a bit 'wet', and you have to be even more careful when folding them through the batter to ensure they don't 'drag' the colour (unless you want swirly blue muffins!). You can also add the zest of a lemon when adding the dry ingredients (for a refreshing zing) or swap the blueberries for raspberries, if preferred.

Benefits: Oats are a good source of fibre and help lower cholesterol. Blueberries are high in antioxidants and rich in vitamin K, which helps promote bone health and heart health. If using plant-based yoghurt, opt for fortified options to ensure you don't miss out on key nutrients.

175g fresh blueberries
200g plain flour
50g rolled oats
2 tsp baking powder
½ tsp bicarbonate of soda
2 tsp vanilla extract
*1 medium-sized very ripe banana (peeled weight around
    125g), mashed*

Dark chocolate and coconut energy balls (page 88) and No-bake fruit and oat bars (page 90)

Sweet potato fritters
(page 139)

Butterbean shakshuka
(page 141)

Tuna niçoise salad
(page 181)

Pesto pasta Buddha
bowl (page 168)

Vegetable noodle
stir fry (page 216)

Herby cod with crispy
potato traybake
(page 210)

Pear and almond traybake
(page 238) with Lemon, ginger
and honey tea (page 107)

125g yoghurt of your choice
100ml vegetable oil
75g maple syrup

1. Preheat the oven to 200°C/180°C fan. Line a 12-hole muffin tin with paper cases and set aside.

2. Tip the blueberries into a small bowl and sprinkle over 1 tbsp of the weighed flour. Toss gently to coat and set aside.

3. In a large mixing bowl, mix together the remaining flour, oats, baking powder, bicarbonate of soda and vanilla extract. Add the mashed banana and mix again.

4. In a separate jug, whisk together the yoghurt, vegetable oil and maple syrup until combined.

5. Pour the wet ingredients into the dry ingredients and mix until completely combined and no lumps remain – you should have a fairly thick batter.

6. Gently fold in the blueberries until evenly distributed through-out the batter, making sure you don't have any lumps of flour remaining either.

7. Divide the mix equally between the prepared muffin cases. Bake in the oven for 20–25 minutes – or until well risen, golden and the surface springs back when lightly touched.

8. Leave to cool in the tins for 5 minutes before transferring to a wire rack to cool for at least 20 minutes – or until cool enough to handle.

Storage: These are best enjoyed fresh, but will keep in an airtight container for up to three days. Can be frozen for up to three months.

OVERNIGHT OATS – FOUR WAYS

Vegan adaptable • **Makes:** 1 bowl
Prep time: 10 minutes, plus at least 4 hours soaking time
(can be prepped the night before)

Overnight oats are super convenient as you can make them the night before, pop them into a bowl, jar or tupperware and chill for up to four days (perfect for batch cooking when you want to get organised for a busy week ahead). There are many flavour combinations to try, so it never gets repetitive – plus it offers the perfect opportunity to include a wide variety of plant-based, fibre-packed foods to help support gut health. In this recipe, I have included my top four flavours for overnight oats. Remember though, if opting for plant-based milk and yoghurt, always choose a fortified variety to ensure you don't miss out on key vitamins and minerals.

Benefits: Oats are a good source of fibre, help lower cholesterol and support overall heart health. Milk and yoghurt provide protein (particularly soya and dairy), as well as calcium and iodine – if you're using a plant milk, make sure these minerals are added.

For the overnight oats base recipe
40g rolled oats
120ml milk of your choice
100g plain yoghurt of your choice
10g seeds, for example chia, sunflower or pumpkin (optional)

For overnight oats toppings and flavours

1. *Banana and peanut butter overnight oats*

   ½ ripe banana, sliced (e.g. medium-sized) – best added in
      the morning to prevent browning
   1 tbsp peanut butter, or nut butter of your choice
   Pinch of ground cinnamon, or to taste

2. *Very berry overnight oats*

   80g fresh or frozen mixed berries (such as strawberries,
      blueberries, raspberries)
   1 tbsp pumpkin seeds
   1 tbsp raisins or sultanas

3. *Apple cinnamon overnight oats*

   ½ small apple, grated
   1 tbsp chopped dried figs or apricots
   1 tbsp chopped nuts (such as almonds or Brazil nuts)
   Pinch of ground cinnamon, or to taste

4. *Carrot cake overnight oats*

   1 small carrot, grated
   1 tbsp raisins or sultanas
   1 tbsp chopped nuts (such as walnuts or pecans)
   Pinch of ground cinnamon

1. Combine all of the base recipe ingredients in a jar or other
   container and mix well.

2. Add your toppings (choose from the options listed in the
   Ingredients section) – you can leave them on top or stir
   through the mixture, according to personal preference.

3. Cover and refrigerate overnight (or for at least 4 hours).

4. When ready to serve, stir well and add a splash more milk, if you wish, to achieve your preferred consistency, add extra toppings, if desired, and enjoy!

Storage: Best made at least four hours in advance, then covered and chilled in the fridge for up to four days.

SWEET POTATO FRITTERS

Vegetarian • **Makes:** 12 fritters – serves 3 to 4 people
Prep time: 15 minutes • **Cook time:** 25–30 minutes

These sweet potato fritters are ideal when you have a little more time in the morning – for example on a weekend for brunch. If you make more than you need, you'll have some for mid-week too! This recipe is packed full of flavour as well as plant-based foods, making it ideal for encouraging gut diversity. I like to make a big batch to keep in my freezer for when I need a quick, nutritious breakfast, stress-free lunch (served with a salad) or simple snack (with a dip). Top with a poached egg for breakfast.

Benefits: Sweet potatoes contain beta-carotene, an antioxidant which is converted into vitamin A in the body, alongside antioxidants like vitamin C and manganese, which can help to protect against oxidative stress and reduce the risk of diseases.

Top tip: If you have a food processor, use the grating attachment to save time when preparing the sweet potatoes and courgette.

Olive oil (decanted into a spray bottle is ideal)
2 medium sweet potatoes, peeled and grated (about 340g grated weight)
1 medium courgette, grated roughly (about 160g grated weight)
80g sweetcorn
100g feta cheese, crumbled
2 tsp smoked paprika
4 garlic cloves, peeled and crushed
Zest of 1 lemon
¼ tsp dried chilli flakes (optional)
2 small to medium eggs, or 1 large egg
100g plain flour

1. Preheat the oven to 220°C/ 200°C fan. Line a baking tray with non-stick baking paper and spray with oil.

2. Place the grated sweet potatoes and courgette into a colander set over the sink. Squeeze out as much liquid as possible (the more liquid you squeeze out, the better the fritters will hold their shape). Place into a large bowl.

3. Add the sweetcorn, crumbled feta cheese, smoked paprika, crushed garlic, lemon zest and chilli flakes (optional), and mix well to combine.

4. In a small bowl, beat the eggs using a fork before adding them to the grated vegetable mix, along with the flour. Mix well to combine.

5. Using 2 tablespoons (though you may find it easier to shape with your hands), make about 12 equal-sized patties, then place each patty onto the prepared baking tray. Flatten the patties slightly, and spray with a little extra oil.

6. Bake in the oven for 25–30 minutes, or until crisp and golden on the outside and cooked completely through on the inside. Use a spatula or palette knife to gently turn the patties halfway through cooking. For crispier patties, cook in a non-stick frying pan (that has been sprayed with a little oil), over medium heat for about 5–7 minutes on each side (make sure the base of the patty is fully cooked and comes away easily before turning).

7. Serve 3 to 4 warm patties with poached eggs for breakfast – or with salad and a dip for lunch or as a snack.

Storage: Serve warm immediately after cooking, or leave to cool before covering and chilling in the fridge for up to three days before reheating. Alternatively, freeze for up to three months.

BUTTERBEAN SHAKSHUKA

Vegetarian • **Serves:** 2 people • **Prep time:** 10 minutes
Cook time: 40 minutes

This comforting butterbean shakshuka is full of protein and fibre, which will help keep you satisfied until your next meal. It's a delicious one-pan option for a weekend brunch, nutritious lunch or supper when you have the time to cook. You can change up this recipe by choosing different beans and pulses (chickpeas work well) or by adjusting the spices to suit your taste. You can also add a handful of spinach when adding the pulses to increase the veggies. I like to serve this dish with a warm flatbread or some crusty bread for dipping (and to mop up the deliciously smoky sauce).

Benefits: Butterbeans are a good source of fibre and protein – and they also count as one of your five a day. Eggs provide additional protein and choline, a mineral that is important for brain health, and are a great example of a vegetarian 'complete protein', because they contain all the essential amino acids your body needs for optimum health.

For the shakshuka
2 tbsp olive oil
1 onion, chopped
1 red, yellow or orange pepper, chopped
4 garlic cloves, crushed
1 tsp ground cumin
2 tsp smoked paprika, or to taste
400g tin of chopped tomatoes
400g tin of butterbeans, drained and rinsed
Salt and freshly ground black pepper, to taste
2 to 4 eggs, depending on appetite

To serve
Freshly chopped coriander, to taste
Yoghurt or crumbled feta cheese (optional)
Dried chilli flakes, to taste
Zest of 1 lemon
Flatbread, or warm crusty bread

1. Heat the olive oil in a deep-set frying pan over medium heat.

2. Add the onion and pepper to the pan and cook for about 10–12 minutes, stirring often, until the vegetables start to soften.

3. Add the garlic, ground cumin and paprika and cook for about 1 minute, stirring often, until fragrant.

4. Pour in the chopped tomatoes and drained butterbeans, stir well and bring to a simmer.

5. Simmer for about 10–15 minutes, stirring occasionally, until the sauce thickens slightly. Season to taste, adding more paprika if desired.

6. Using the back of a large spoon, make 2–4 wells in the sauce (depending on how many eggs you intend to cook), then crack an egg into each one.

7. Continue to cook for about 5–7 minutes, or until the egg whites are set but the yolks are still runny (cover with a lid, if you have one, to speed up the process – just watch closely to ensure the eggs don't overcook). Once the eggs are cooked to your liking, remove the pan from the heat.

8. Garnish the shakshuka with coriander, yoghurt or feta cheese, chilli flakes (optional) and lemon zest. Season with salt and pepper. Serve straight away with warm crusty bread or flatbread (you can present the shakshuka family-style, or dish it up onto individual lipped plates).

Storage: Once you have cooked the eggs in the sauce, this dish is best served immediately. If you want to prepare your shakshuka in advance, you can make the sauce base by following steps 1–5 of the method shown, then transferring it to a tupperware to cool before covering and chilling in the fridge for up to three days. When you are ready to serve the dish, simply return the sauce base to a pan, bring it to a simmer, then proceed with steps 6–8 of the recipe. Alternatively, you can just reheat the base, then top with poached eggs that have been cooked separately.

END OF WEEK 2 (BREAKFAST) REFLECTION

Time to get your journal out (or to take a moment) to reflect on your week. Note down or think about any successes or setbacks you had, as acknowledging these is important in order to grow and improve.

Reflection questions

Have a think about your answers to the following questions:

- **Did you eat breakfast every day?** (There is no correct answer to this, however if you noticed that skipping breakfast impacted your choices later in the morning or in the afternoon then you may want to plan to have easy to grab breakfasts ready each day.)

- **Were your meals balanced?** That is, did they contain carbohydrates (fibre), protein and healthy fats?

- **Did your breakfasts include fruits or vegetables?** To get an early start on reaching your five servings a day.

- **How satisfied did you feel after breakfast**? Did you include enough protein and fibre?

- **Did you choose any UPF items for breakfast?** If so, how frequently and why?

- **Did you manage to reduce your UPF intake at breakfast time?** How did you do this?

- **How were your energy levels after breakfast?** Compare a UPF morning versus a non-UPF morning, if you can.

- **How did your breakfast choices influence your mid-morning snacking patterns?**

- **What were your main challenges in making healthier breakfast choices?**

Now you know the areas that you want to work on regarding your breakfasts, what is the first action you want to take? Make a note of it in your food diary and work on it over the following week while we take a look at your lunch options in week 3.

CHAPTER 7

WEEK 3 – LUNCHES

I n today's busy age, lunch on the go is the norm, making it a magnet for UPFs. Eating UPFs – especially the less-nutri-tious kind – in the middle of the day can lead to unsustained energy levels and the dreaded afternoon slump. Depending on how you currently navigate lunch, this week may or may not require more changes than you made in weeks 1 and 2, but just like in previous chapters, I will walk you through, step by step, how to both increase the nutritional density of your diet and reduce the number of UPFs you consume.

Lunch, your midday meal (also known as 'dinner' to many), is an opportunity to not only take a break, but to re-energise ourselves through food. In some countries, such as Spain, lunch is a much more respected time, with a generous two to three hours given to prepare food, eat and even take a rest, which means food can be digested before returning to work. In countries like the UK, however, lunch is often an afterthought following back-to-back meetings, and is something that many people eat on the go or at their desk. With tired brains, the last thing we want to do is think about how we can construct an affordable but healthy lunch from a handful of raw ingredients – let alone think about what utensils are available in the staff kitchen (in my time spent working for the NHS, I remember there was always a distinct lack of forks). We crave convenience, ease and comfort, such as a slice of pizza from the shop next door, or a quick coffee and a dough-nut as we dash to our next port of call.

But it doesn't have to be this way. In this chapter, I am going to show you how lunchtime can be a more peaceful pause to nour-ish yourself, and how it can make the afternoon as productive as it can be, with a shift in mindset.

The key, as always, is prepping and making conscious decisions. For me, lunchtime is often 'something nutritious on toast', or left-overs, but options can be limited if you don't have a fridge or microwave at work (for example, if you're on the road all day). This is why we will explore lots of different options, so no matter what your circumstances are, there will be a healthy lunch that's right for you. As with breakfast, it is important that our meals are balanced and contain both vegetables and lean proteins to properly fuel, in addition to slow-release carbohydrates (prefer-ably wholegrain) and healthy fats too.

To-do lists are often long, but the reality is that they will only keep getting longer, so setting boundaries – for example taking at least 15 minutes to step away from your desk – is crucial, not only for stress management and a change of perspective, but to fuel ourselves mindfully too. For this reason, I urge you to put a lunch break into your diary as an appointment with yourself, just as you would a meeting.

A lovely patient of mine who worked from home explained that she didn't take a lunch break, so that she could finish her day 15 minutes earlier instead. On reflection, she realised that this led to her grazing from the kitchen for the majority of the day, which left her feeling neither refreshed nor satisfied. I urged her to change her working pattern for the sake of her health, and to plan in time away from her desk, to get some daylight and to have a decent lunch too.

She decided that she could prepare a lunch either the night before or in the morning before starting work. Where there is a will, there is a way! You deserve a break, so take it. You are not a robot.

NON-UPF VS UPF EXAMPLES AT LUNCH

Let's focus on a popular go-to lunch option, the sandwich.

Although they can make a perfectly healthy lunch choice, a typical pre-packaged sandwich from supermarkets or coffee shops is classed as a UPF. You can spot this immediately, as the ingredients lists for these sandwiches are usually long, filled with words that are often hard to pronounce and substances that are not usually found in a typical kitchen. They may include various additives such as preservatives, emulsifiers and artificial flavours, designed to prolong shelf life and enhance taste. For instance, a turkey salad sandwich might contain modified starches to stabilise the sauce, added sugars to enhance flavour and preservatives like sodium nitrate to keep the turkey looking tasty. Even though it does contain some salad, the ratio of salad to other ingredients is often pretty poor (as is usually evident by looking through the little plastic window!).

There is a time and place for meal-deal sandwiches – if you didn't have time to prepare lunch and you find yourself hungry in town between meetings, for example – however you don't want them to make up the majority of your lunches in a week. If you are opting for a pre-made sandwich, look for ones that will provide more micronutrients (vitamins, minerals and antioxidants) and fibre, meaning something with plenty of salad and wholegrain bread, and those that contain plant-based protein such as hummus or falafel, or lean meat.

The best option for health when it comes to sandwiches is always going to be making your own – carving out just ten minutes in a morning to take charge of what's going into your freshly made lunch could have a huge impact on your health, especially when done on a regular basis. And it's not just about the sandwich, it's the drink and sides that come with a meal-deal sandwich, too – so packing a bottle of water and some fruit will not only help to reduce your UPF intake, but will reduce your free-sugar intake and increase your nutrient intake too. Plus, it will also save you money.

Make your own sandwich or wrap and you can choose a non-UPF bread and lean protein source such as falafel or even last night's leftover roasted chicken. Additions like avocado for healthy fats and rocket or salad leaves will give you more nutrients that contribute to fullness levels too.

Non-UPF lunch examples	More-nutritious or less energy-dense UPF lunch examples	Less-nutritious or more energy-dense UPF lunch examples
Homemade chicken salad (non-UPF) wrap* with an apple and water	Shop-bought chicken salad sandwich on brown bread with pineapple chunks and water	Shop-bought BLT sandwich, ready salted crisps and cola
Wholegrain (non-UPF) bagel* with avocado, eggs and salmon	Pre-packaged bagel with cream cheese and salmon from coffee shop	Shop-bought bagel with sausages and ketchup, plus a chocolate muffin and fizzy drink
Homemade tomato and lentil soup with non-UPF wholemeal or traditionally made sourdough bread*	Supermarket tomato soup (found in the chiller section) with any wholemeal bread	Microwavable pizza and chips (from supermarket) or takeaway pizza and chips
Chicken and quinoa salad, homemade, with lemon and olive oil dressing	Shop-bought tomato and basil pasta salad	Shop-bought chicken pasta salad box loaded with mayonnaise (minimal salad ingredients)

_____

For wraps, bagels and breads to be non-UPF they should not contain emulsifiers – simply wheat (with added vitamins if it's a white loaf) or rye (or other grain), water and salt, plus other optional whole-food ingredients such as seeds.

HOW TO CHOOSE BETWEEN TWO UPF LUNCHES

Let's look at the nutritional differences between two of the meal deal examples listed in the table.

Meal deal 1 (less-nutritious UPF) – BLT sandwich, cola and salted crisps

Sandwich ingredients – Wheat Flour [**Wheat** Flour, Calcium Carbonate, Iron, Niacin, Thiamin], Chicken Breast (23%), Water, Smoked Bacon (12%) [Pork Belly, Sugar, Salt, Emulsifier (Sodium Triphosphate), Honey, Preservative (Sodium Nitrite)], Lettuce, Malted **Wheat** Flakes, Rapeseed Oil, **Wheat** Bran, Cornflour, Salt, **Wheat** Gluten, Malted **Barley** Flour, White Wine Vinegar, Yeast, Pasteurised **Egg** Yolk, Emulsifiers (Mono- and Di-Glycerides of Fatty Acids, Mono- and Di-Acetyl Tartaric Acid Esters of Mono- and Di-Glycerides of Fatty Acids), Spirit Vinegar, Malted **Wheat** Flour, **Mustard** Flour, Black Pepper, Garlic Powder, Flour Treatment Agent (Ascorbic Acid), Palm Oil, Sunflower Oil.

Contains 435 kcal (22%), 17.3g fat (25%), 4.8 g saturates (24%), 6.1g sugar (7%), 2.23g salt (37%), 5.2 g fibre (17%).

500ml bottle of cola ingredients – Carbonated Water, Sugar, Colour (Caramel E150d), Acid (Phosphoric Acid), Natural Flavourings including Caffeine.

Contains 210 kcal (11%), 0g fat, 0g saturates, 53g sugar (59%*), 0g salt, 0g fibre.

---

* This is of our total daily sugar allowance (90g), which includes sugars from fruit and milk too. In reality though, it is 177% of our daily free-sugar (or added sugar) allowance, which is just 30g.

Crisps (baked, sea salt) ingredients – *Potato Flakes, Starch, Rapeseed Oil, Sugar, Emulsifier (Lecithins), Sea Salt Seasonings (Sea Salt, Salt Flavourings), Sunflower Oil, Colour (Annatto Norbixin).*

Contains 164 kcal (8%), 4.8g fat (7%), 0.5g saturates (3%), 2g sugar (2%), salt 0.32g (5%), fibre 2.4g (8%)

Meal deal 2 (more-nutritious UPF) – chicken salad sandwich on brown bread with pineapple chunks and water

Sandwich ingredients – *Chicken Breast (29%), Wheat Flour [**Wheat** Flour, Calcium Carbonate, Iron, Niacin, Thiamin], Water, Tomato, Cucumber, Lettuce, Malted **Wheat** Flakes, Rapeseed Oil, Cornflour, **Wheat** Bran, Lemon Juice, Salt, White Wine Vinegar, Malted **Barley** Flour, Yeast, Emulsifiers (Mono- and Di-Glycerides of Fatty Acids, Mono- and Di-Acetyl Tartaric Acid Esters of Mono- and Di-Glycerides of Fatty Acids), **Wheat** Gluten, Spirit Vinegar, Pasteurised **Egg** Yolk, Malted **Wheat** Flour, Black Pepper, Citrus Fibre, Garlic Powder, **Mustard** Flour, Flour Treatment Agent (Ascorbic Acid), Palm Oil, Sunflower Oil.*

Contains 361 kcal (18%), 6.1g fat (9%), 1g saturates (5%), 4.5g sugar (5%), 1.1g salt (18%) 4.7g fibre (16%)

Pineapple chunk ingredients – *100% Pineapple*

Contains 72 kcal (4%), fat 0.1g (<1%), 0g saturates, sugars 16g (18%), salt 0.01g (<1%), fibre 1.7g (6%)

Water ingredients – *100% Natural mineral water*

Contains 0 kcal

Here are the total calorie, fat, saturated fat, sugars, salt and fibre stats for comparison:

Meal deal 1 (less-nutritious UPF option) – *809 kcal (40%), 22.1g fat (32%), 5.3g saturates (27%), 61.1g sugar (68%), 2.55g salt (43%), 7.6g fibre (25%)*

Meal deal 2 (more-nutritious UPF option) – *433 kcal (22%), 6.2g fat (9%), 1g saturates (5%), 20.5g sugars (23%), 1.1g salt (19%), 6.4g fibre (21%)*

The first meal deal option is a popular choice for many, but it is extremely high in salt and is lacking in salad and vegetables. The BLT sandwich alone contributes a whopping 37 per cent of the maximum daily salt recommendations, which is a substantial portion, especially coming from just one food item – add the crisps and it takes it to over 40 per cent of an entire day's allowance for salt.

Choosing full-sugar cola over water also boosts your added sugar intake by 53g, which could lead to a rapid rise in blood sugar levels, especially if consumed on an empty stomach. Swapping to the diet (sugar-free) version, while still a UPF, reduces your added sugar intake dramatically, which may be a good compromise until you feel ready to swap to water for the majority of your lunchtimes.

Regarding meal-deal sides, while many crisps contain just potatoes, oil and salt, this 'baked' bag contains way more additives (to make them lower in fat, which some people see as being more attractive in a snack), and adds more salt to the meal too, in addition to being extremely nutrient poor. Crisps (and chocolate bars!) are typical less-nutritious UPF sides, providing easy to eat and moreish calories primarily from refined carbohydrates and fats, with minimal fibre, which means less overall fullness and nourishment. Now let's take a look at a homemade chicken sandwich ingredients list:

Homemade chicken salad sandwich ingredients – *Chicken breast on wholegrain bread [wholewheat flour, water, yeast, salt] with tomato, cucumber and lettuce, with a dressing of extra virgin olive oil, lemon juice and black pepper.*

Plus an apple and water.

This homemade chicken salad sandwich not only has a much shorter ingredients list, thanks to no emulsifiers and additives, but it has much less salt and fat, in particular saturated fat, in comparison to the BLT sandwich. Prepare a sandwich at home and not only can you control what goes in it, but you can select your own sides too – fruit or plain yoghurt and water will provide hydration and fibre, as well as essential nutrients, such as vitamin C and calcium.

It's a no-brainer that having a homemade lunch is always going to be the best for our health in the long term, and it is one of the easiest ways to reduce your intake of UPFs. However if you are caught short and need to buy a pre-packaged sandwich, spend a few moments looking at the ingredients lists of the meal-deal options on offer, and try choosing ones with more whole foods and less in the way of additives.

WHAT ARE THE COMMON PROBLEMS WITH UPFs AT LUNCHTIME?

The aim of your midday meal should be to set you up for the afternoon, and to provide a steady release of energy and nutrients to get you through until mid or late afternoon (when a snack or your next meal will be due). The issue with not finding, or making, the time to make homemade lunches (even a container of leftovers!) is that you're likely to find yourself with an increased intake of UPFs. Even canteens that provide freshly cooked foods usually offer plenty of tempting UPFs to go alongside them.

Having a meal high in UPFs, particularly the less-nutritious kind, could lead to an energy roller coaster, and possibly food-seeking behaviours in the afternoon too – for example, a highly processed ham sandwich on white bread with a packet of crisps and a cola may not provide you with sustained energy, thus leaving you vulnerable to 'head hunger' or food cravings in the afternoon, resulting in you picking on those office buns you resisted in the morning.

The key is preparation and nourishing your body at each meal time, including lunch. Making more than what you need at dinner will mean an easy lunch the following day, or aim to prepare something the night before or in the morning, using whole foods including wholegrains, lean proteins, healthy fats and plenty of fruits and vegetables, too. This combination of food will provide a steady source of energy, keeping blood sugar levels stable and preventing any mid-afternoon slump. Once you've got into the habit of preparing lunch instead of relying on UPFs, you can then look to increase the diversity of ingredients used to improve your health even further. The more diverse the range of foods you eat, the more diverse the range of nutrients you will get and the better your gut microbes will function, which may impact not only your digestive health, but your mood and immune system too.

Instead of saying, 'I don't have time to make my lunch', say to yourself, 'I'm not prioritising making my lunch', or, 'Making my lunch isn't a priority for me right now' – this is OK now and again, but hearing this may help give you the motivation to move things around so that you *can* make time to make it. Remember the motto 'cook once, eat twice' when it comes to preparing your next meal, and it will make meal preparation even faster the next day (in other words, cook more than you need so you can have it the following day too). Today, choose to also help out the future you too.

TOP TIPS TO MAKE LUNCHTIME LESS ABOUT UPFs AND MUCH MORE NUTRITIOUS

The following are suggestions that will help to not only reduce your overall intake of UPFs, but increase your nutrient intake too. Depending on the day, your food and drink choices will change, but the key, as always, is to make sure that you are making informed decisions.

- **Choose the most nutritious meal-deal main with non-UPF sides and drink:** if you have to choose a meal-deal sandwich, choose one loaded with salad and ideally on wholemeal bread, with a lean protein. Choose fruit as the side and water, or at the very least an unsweetened drink (or diet drink if you must!).

- **Learn to love leftovers:** cooking extra food at your evening meal for lunch the following day can not only save money, but also means you have a home-cooked nutrient-dense meal, free from UPFs. If it can be eaten cold then great, but if not, have a look into the food flasks that you can buy that keep heated food hot for several hours – they work in the same way that drinks flasks keep hot drinks hot!

- **Meal prep your lunches:** if you're taking the time to make one lunch then why not make two? Other time-saving tips include prepping ingredients ahead of time (for example, shredding carrot and slicing cucumber, which can then be stored in an airtight container in the fridge) for a quick and simple addition to salads, wraps and sandwiches.

- **Make your own salad dressings:** come up with a couple of simple homemade dressings like vinegar with lemon juice, black pepper and olive oil to boost the flavour and also nutrient absorption of veggies and salads (the vitamins A, D, E and K require fats to be absorbed). You don't have to rely on UPF dressings from the supermarket to make your salads tasty.

- **Experiment with fermented foods:** the key to healthy eating is variety, as well as eating plenty of plants. Fermented foods such as kimchi (fermented vegetables), sauerkraut (fermented cabbage) or even kefir (a fermented milk drink) are known for their probiotic benefits, essential for gut health, and can make an interesting addition to a packed lunch.

HEALTHY NON-UPF LUNCH IDEAS

It can be helpful to think about lunch ideas under the following four themes: on toast or a bagel; in a wrap or sandwich; as a soup, salad or omelette; or jacket potatoes and leftovers.

1 On toast or a bagel: some of my favourites are avocado with eggs, or hummus on wholegrain toast with sun-dried tomatoes, accompanied by a side salad or roasted green beans. Make sure the bread you buy is non-UPF, i.e. ensure that it doesn't contain additives such as emulsifiers.

2 **Wraps and sandwiches:** wholegrain wraps and sourdough sandwiches are super versatile and can be a great vehicle for lean proteins and vegetables. I like to fill mine with foods such as grilled chicken or marinated tofu, mixed salad vegetables and a homemade olive oil-based dressing.

3 **Soups, salads and omelettes:** try a quinoa salad (you can buy quinoa precooked in a packet for ease from supermarkets) with mixed roasted vegetables, chopped mixed nuts and an olive oil and lemon dressing, topped with feta cheese and seeds. Or on chillier days, you could batch prepare a delicious lentil soup or omelette.

4 **Jacket potatoes and leftovers:** last night's grilled salmon over a bed of mixed greens and sweet potato mash – delicious! I like to pop jacket potatoes in with leftovers as although you can cook them in the microwave on the day that you want them, they are an ideal food to cook the night before (just pop an extra one in the oven!) and top with whatever you fancy, for example cottage cheese, tuna salad or leftover chilli.

Here are ten lunch ideas that can be prepped and either enjoyed at home or taken with you on the go. I've included five of my favourite recipes at the end of this chapter, too, in case you need further inspiration. You'll notice that each suggestion contains a starchy carbohydrate (ideally wholegrain) for energy and fibre, protein for essential amino acids (the breakdown of protein for growth and repair), a vegetable or salad for micronutrients, and healthy fats – together these make the lunches nutritionally balanced and satisfying too. Which takes your fancy?

1 **Smashed avocado and either eggs, halloumi or scrambled tofu**, on sourdough toast or rye bread with chopped fresh tomatoes and spinach.

2 **Chicken salad wholegrain wrap**, served with fruit and yoghurt as a side.

3 **Wholegrain pasta salad**, with mixed leaves, cooked lentils and feta cheese, topped with a sprinkle of seeds.

4 **Mixed bean salad and brown rice burrito**, with optional chicken and (freshly grated) cheese.

5 **Kale and avocado salad with chicken** and roasted cauliflower with jacket potato.

6 **Hummus and roasted red pepper wrap**, with leafy greens.

7 **Minestrone and vegetable or lentil soup**, served with non-UPF wholemeal or sourdough bread.

8 **Smoked salmon, cream cheese and cucumber on a (non-UPF) wholegrain bagel**, served with a green side salad.

9 **Quinoa salad**, with hummus and roasted peppers.

10 **Omelette**, served with a green salad and a side of toasted sourdough bread.

SHOPPING LIST EASY WINS – YOUR KITCHEN ESSENTIALS FOR A HEALTHY LUNCH

Make lunch at home easier by stocking your kitchen with versatile ingredients to make meal prep easy. The following foods are suggestions to help you make 'on toast' or 'bagel' meals, wraps and sandwiches, soups, salads, omelettes and jacket potatoes quick and easy, and to help you to use up any leftovers from your evening meal the night before. Remember, cook once, eat twice!

Fresh produce and fridge items

- **Fresh berries and mango**, for sides or salads.

- **Beans and courgettes** for fritters.

- **Lettuce, mixed leaves or spinach** for sandwiches and salads.

- **Radishes**, sliced, they make the perfect easy salad toppers.

- **Avocados** for toast and salads – they bring lots of healthy fats to the plate.

- **Eggs**, for on toast options and omelettes.

- **Plain yoghurt**, for sides.

- **Plain chicken**, for cooking and adding to wraps and salads.

- **Fresh salmon**, for salads.

- **Cream cheese or feta cheese**, for toast and salads.

- **Plain tofu**, for scrambling (if you don't eat eggs).

- **Potatoes**, sweet or regular.

- **Hummus (containing whole-food ingredients only)**.

Cupboard items

- **Wholegrain or sourdough bread**, just look for options with a minimal ingredients list.

- **Wholegrain wraps, crackers and bagels**, non-UPF, made from whole foods.

- **Plain bulgur wheat and quinoa**, can buy pre-cooked for ease.

- **Nuts**, such as almonds, walnuts, Brazil nuts, cashews or mixed nuts (plain).

- **Wholegrain pasta and rice**, for hot or cold salads.

- **Tinned chickpeas and beans,** e.g. tinned mixed-bean salad or butter beans for homemade salads.

- **Tinned sweetcorn**, for omelettes and salads.

- **Spices**, such as paprika, dried parsley and chilli flakes for flavour.

- **Nutritional yeast**, for a flavour and nutrient boost – look for varieties with added vitamin B12, especially if you're vegan. (See the Appendix at the end of this book for more information on vitamins and minerals, the addition of which does not make a food a UPF.)

Frozen foods

- **Frozen spinach cubes**, these make great easy additions to soups and pasta sauces.

HOW TO ORGANISE YOUR KITCHEN FOR LUNCH SUCCESS

You've done this twice already, so perhaps you feel very on top of your kitchen by now! But if lunch is a meal you struggle to make UPF-free, consider following these tips:

- Keep your spices organised in their own compartment, motivating yourself to use them so you can cut down on salt.

- Dedicate a section of your fridge to leftover meals (store *above* rather than below any raw meats and fish).

- If leftover meals are freezable (for example chilli), freeze it for future days when you are less motivated – label what it is, as well as the dates that it was cooked and frozen on.

- Bonus, make your food prep area an attractive space – can you add a plant or a picture to brighten up the area? If spaces are attractive, then you'll be more likely to want to be there.

MEAL PLANNER WITH NON-UPF SNACKS, DRINKS, BREAKFASTS AND LUNCHES

Lunchtime can be prone to relying on the shops around you at the time, so packing a healthy lunch is a great idea to keep your UPF intake low, and your wholegrain and vegetable intake high, which can be hard to do in fast food joints. To save on prep time, you could also have leftovers from dinner the previous night, or have the same salad or wrap two days in a row.

	Monday	Tuesday	Wednesday
Breakfast	Overnight oats (see recipe on page 136) with nut butter and banana	Butterbean shakshuka (see recipe on page 141)	Vegan oaty blueberry muffins (see recipe on page 134)
Morning snack	Apple and cheese	Oatcakes topped with nut butter and banana slices	Berries with plain yoghurt and a drizzle of honey if desired
Lunch	Pesto pasta Buddha bowl (see recipe on page 168)	Smashed avocado, feta and eggs on wholegrain bread (see recipe on page 174)	Tuna niçoise salad (see recipe on page 181)
Afternoon snack	Carrots and hummus – homemade (see recipe on page 85) or shop bought	Dark chocolate and coconut energy balls (see recipe on page 88)	Small bag of popcorn – or pop at home with kernels
Evening meal			
Dessert/ evening snack			
Drinks	Water and warm golden milk with turmeric	Water and hot chocolate made from warm milk, cocoa powder and a dash of maple syrup	Water and strawberry-and cucumber-infused water

Week 3 – lunches

Thursday	Friday	Saturday	Sunday
Peanut butter and banana on wholegrain toast	Greek yoghurt pancakes (see recipe on page 132)	Sweet potato fritters (see recipe on page 139)	Spinach and mushroom omelette
Healthy trail mix – made from plain nuts, dried fruit and dark chocolate	Dried apricots and almonds	Medjool dates stuffed with nut butter and a little dark chocolate	Avocado on a wholegrain cracker with slices of boiled egg
Mediterranean mozzarella, pesto and tomato wrap (see recipe on page 179)	Carrot and lentil soup (see recipe on page 177)	Hummus with garlic and herb mushrooms on sourdough toast (see recipe on page 175)	Sunday dinner with all the trimmings
Roasted butter beans with olive oil and spices	No-bake fruit and oat bars (see recipe on page 90)	Pear and a handful of walnuts	Roasted kale crisps
Water and herbal tea of choice	Water and lemon, ginger and honey tea (see recipe on page 107)	Water and fresh carrot and orange juice (see recipe on page 105)	Water and date, banana and cocoa smoothie (see recipe on page 104)

YOUR FIVE-STEP HEALTHY CHECKLIST FOR WEEK 3 (LUNCH)

You know the drill. Changes are made easier when you set goals and have specific tasks to work on. Have a look at the checklist below and decide which you want to focus on for the week ahead, or give it a tick on the right-hand side if you already do it – and congratulate yourself too!

Tick on the left if you want to work on a particular goal, and on the right when you have achieved it:

Tick to work on ✔	Goal	Tick when completed ✔
	Make a homemade lunch (or two!) this week with at least one additional serving of vegetables. The more colours, the better.	
	Choose wholegrains as your lunchtime carb, e.g. wholegrain rice or pasta, wholemeal bread, etc.	
	Make an extra portion of your evening meal to have as leftovers for lunch the next day.	
	Choose fruit as the snack and water as the drink in a meal deal.	
	Eat lunch away from your desk if you work in an office. Bonus – stretch your legs outside and go for a little walk.	

NON-UPF HEALTHY LUNCH RECIPES

Here are five of my favourite healthy lunch recipes either to have at home or for on the go.

- Pesto pasta Buddha bowl

- Lunchtime 'on toast' – four ways

- Carrot and lentil soup

- Mediterranean mozzarella, pesto and tomato wrap

- Tuna niçoise salad

PESTO PASTA BUDDHA BOWL

Vegetarian/vegan adaptable* • **Serves:** 2 people
Prep time: 10 minutes • **Cook time:** 25 minutes

Pesto pasta is a simple yet delicious dish. In my version, you will see that by adding just a few plant-based ingredients, you can create a nutrient-packed, nourishing meal that tastes good and sets you well on your way to eating your five a day. It is also a really versatile recipe as you can swap the chickpeas for all sorts of beans (butterbeans or cannellini beans work well), alter the veggies depending on what you already have (beetroot, grated courgette and sweetcorn are all ideal additions) and work your way through the different hummus flavours that are included in Chapter 5 (Week 1 – snacks and drinks) of this book. You can even add a sprinkling of toasted chopped nuts or seeds for extra fibre, healthy fats and texture, if desired, and include cooked chicken if you eat meat. There is also lots of flexibility in the ingredients that can be used in the pesto. While pine nuts are the traditional choice for pesto, they can be expensive, so I like to mix it up by using other nuts from time to time, too.

Benefits: Wholegrain pasta, chickpeas and vegetables provide fibre and allow for the slow release of energy, which will help keep you satisfied for longer.

Top tip: Double up on ingredients so your lunch is sorted for the next few days. You will have some crunchy paprika chickpeas left over – I like to enjoy them as a healthy snack or to add them to soups.

---

* If making for vegetarians, use a vegetarian Italian-style hard cheese. If making for vegans, use a vegan alternative.

For the homemade pesto
(quantities can be doubled to make extra)
15g almonds, cashew nuts or pine nuts
30g fresh basil
30g Parmesan cheese/vegetarian cheese or vegan
    alternative, finely grated
2 garlic cloves
60ml extra virgin olive oil
Zest of 1 lemon, optional

For the Buddha bowl
150g uncooked wholegrain penne pasta, or alternative
    pasta shape of your choice
400g can chickpeas, drained and rinsed
1 tbsp olive oil
1 tsp paprika, or to taste
Salt and freshly ground black pepper, to taste
½ cucumber, chopped into small pieces
2 carrots, grated
1 roasted red pepper, thinly sliced
2 handfuls of fully prepared, washed and ready-to-eat
    mixed salad leaves or spinach
150g (approximately 10) cherry tomatoes or baby plum
    tomatoes, halved
About 150g cooked chicken, sliced or shredded (optional)
2–4 tbsp hummus (see the recipe for my 'Healthy hummus –
    four ways' in Chapter 5 [Week 1 – snacks and drinks] for my
    homemade hummus recipe)

1. Preheat the oven to 200°C/180°C fan.

For the homemade pesto

2. Place the nuts, basil, Parmesan cheese (or alternative)
    and garlic cloves into a mini blender and pulse until finely

chopped. Gradually add the oil, blitzing until you have achieved your desired consistency. Add lemon zest (optional), then taste and adjust the seasoning as necessary.

For the Buddha bowl

3. Cook the pasta according to packet instructions. Drain and run under cold water to stop the cooking process. Set aside.

4. Tip the drained and rinsed chickpeas into a large bowl. Drizzle over the oil, dust with paprika and season with salt, to taste. Mix well to coat. Tip onto a baking sheet and spread in an even layer. Roast in the oven for 20–25 minutes, turning halfway through, or until crunchy.

5. Tip the pasta into a bowl and stir through 3–4 tablespoons of the homemade pesto. Season to taste.

6. Spoon a portion of the pesto pasta into the middle of your serving bowl. Arrange the cucumber, carrot, pepper, mixed salad leaves, cherry tomatoes, roasted chickpeas and shredded chicken (if using) around the pesto pasta. Top with a generous dollop of hummus, and enjoy!

Storage: The individual components can be made separately, and can be covered and chilled in the fridge for up to three days.

LUNCHTIME 'ON TOAST' – FOUR WAYS

Vegetarian and vegan adaptable options
Each variation serves: 1 • **Prep time:** approximately 10 minutes
• **Cook time:** varies depending on options chosen

'On toast' recipes are one of my go-tos for a quick and simple mid-week lunch, either in the office or at home. I have included some of my favourite recipes here – they can all be served as an open sandwich, and some can be placed together and popped in a tupperware box for a delicious and nutritious lunch on the go (just make sure you use a non-UPF bread such as sourdough). All of my 'on toast' variations are designed to be quick and simple – without the use of an oven. I have included a cheese, fish, egg and vegan option – so there are plenty of ideas to choose from!

Benefits: Choose wholegrain breads, where possible, for extra fibre and B vitamins. Seeded breads offer more plant-based diversity and healthy fats too, although look for varieties without any additives such as emulsifiers.

1.
GOAT'S CHEESE, FIGS AND HONEY ON TOAST

Vegetarian (ensure your cheese is vegetarian-friendly and doesn't have animal rennet)

This French-inspired recipe is so easy to make and is full of flavour. It is also very flexible – if you aren't a fan of goat's cheese, you can use cottage cheese for a milder flavour. On the other hand, a soft blue cheese like Dolcelatte is also delicious if you like stronger flavours. I add a sprinkling of toasted walnuts and hazelnuts for crunch, but you can omit if you prefer. You can also make smaller toasts and serve as a canapé if you have friends and family over. Cheese is a good source of protein, while nuts provide healthy fats and fibre.

*1 to 2 slices of bread (ideally traditionally made sourdough
   or non-UPF wholemeal or seeded)*
65g soft goat's cheese
2 ripe fresh figs, sliced
A pinch of freshly plucked thyme leaves
Toasted walnuts or hazelnuts, for sprinkling (optional)
A drizzle of runny honey
Freshly ground black pepper
*A handful of fully prepared washed and ready-to-eat rocket
   or watercress*

1. Toast 1–2 slices of bread and set on a plate, then spread with the soft goat's cheese.

2. Arrange the fig slices on top.

3. Sprinkle with freshly plucked thyme leaves.

4. Roughly chop the walnuts or hazelnuts, if using, and scatter over the slices.

5. Drizzle with honey and season with freshly ground black pepper, to taste. Add a handful of rocket or watercress to the side of the plate and enjoy.

2.
SMOKED MACKEREL PÂTÉ
AND CUCUMBER ON TOAST

This zesty mackerel pâté is unbelievably easy to make and takes just minutes to bring together (it is also brilliant for when you have guests over, and it works equally well as a dip with toasted pitta bread). Mackerel is an excellent source of omega-3s, which help keep your heart and brain healthy.

For the mackerel pâté (you will have extra)
200g ready-to-eat smoked mackerel fillets
125g soft cheese or plain Greek yoghurt (I use 0% with oily fish)
1 lemon, zested and juiced
Salt and freshly ground black pepper, to taste
2 tbsp fresh roughly chopped parsley or finely sliced chives

To serve
1 to 2 slices of bread (ideally traditionally made sourdough or non-UPF wholemeal or seeded)
2–3 tbsp homemade mackerel pâté per slice
¼ of a medium-sized cucumber, sliced
Fresh roughly chopped parsley or finely sliced chives
A handful of fully prepared washed and ready-to-eat rocket or watercress

1. Remove the skin from the mackerel and tip into a medium-sized bowl or small food processor if you have one. Break the fillets up into small pieces. Add the soft cheese and lemon zest and mix well with a fork (if mixing by hand) or blitz (if using a food processor).

2. Season with salt and freshly ground black pepper, to taste, and add a squeeze of lemon juice. Taste and adjust

accordingly. Mix well again. Spoon into an airtight container and chill until ready to serve (or for up to 3 days).

3. When ready to serve: toast 1–2 slices of bread and set on a plate. Spread with the homemade mackerel pâté.

4. Arrange the sliced cucumber on top and sprinkle with your choice of herbs. Add a handful of rocket or watercress to the side of the plate and enjoy.

3.
SMASHED AVOCADO, FETA AND EGGS ON TOAST

Vegetarian

This is one of my go-to recipes when I want a quick and simple meal that is packed full of nutrients (it is equally delicious for breakfast, brunch, lunch or supper). The avocados are an excellent source of healthy fats and fibre, the feta provides calcium and the eggs are a complete protein. I like to serve this with boiled or poached eggs (I cook my boiled eggs to the 'jammy' stage so that the yolk is still runny in the centre) – but scrambled eggs are also delicious. This is best served straight away, rather than eating on the go.

1 small ripe avocado
Juice of 1 lemon
1 to 2 slices of bread (ideally traditionally made sourdough or non-UPF wholemeal or seeded)
7 cherry or baby plum tomatoes, halved
2 eggs – your choice of boiled (I liked medium-soft boiled) and peeled/poached/scrambled

30g feta
Pinch of chilli flakes (optional)
Sesame seeds, to sprinkle (optional)
Extra virgin olive oil, to drizzle (optional)

1. Cut the avocado in half and carefully remove the stone. Scoop out the flesh into a bowl and add the lemon juice, to taste. Mash with a fork to your desired texture.

2. Toast 1–2 slices of bread and set on a plate.

3. Spoon the smashed avocado onto the toast and spread in an even layer. Arrange the tomatoes on top, followed by the eggs.

4. Crumble over the feta and sprinkle with chilli flakes and sesame seeds (if using). Drizzle with extra virgin olive oil, if desired, and serve.

4.
HUMMUS WITH GARLIC AND HERB MUSHROOMS ON TOAST

Vegan

This recipe is the perfect example of how you can pack multiple plant-based foods into one meal (you can also add a handful of spinach when cooking the mushrooms, if you like). Mushrooms provide B vitamins, while hummus is packed with protein and fibre.

1 tbsp olive oil, plus extra for drizzling (optional)
125g chestnut mushrooms, trimmed and sliced
1–2 garlic cloves, crushed

Your choice of herbs: a couple of sprigs of freshly plucked thyme/1–2 tbsp roughly chopped coriander or parsley/a pinch of dried mixed herbs

Salt and freshly ground black pepper, to taste

1 to 2 slices of bread (ideally traditionally made sourdough or non-UPF wholemeal or seeded)

2–3 tbsp hummus (see the recipe for my 'Healthy hummus – four ways' in Chapter 5 [Week 1 – snacks and drinks] for my homemade hummus recipe)

A handful of fully prepared, washed and ready-to-eat rocket or watercress

Toasted pine nuts or sesame seeds, for sprinkling (optional)

1. Heat the oil in a medium-sized frying pan and cook the mushrooms over a medium heat for 5 minutes, stirring often, or until they start to turn golden. Add the garlic and cook for another minute or so.

2. Add your choice of herbs, mix gently and season with salt and pepper, to taste. Reduce the heat to low and keep warm.

3. Toast 1–2 slices of bread and set on a plate. Spread with the hummus.

4. Spoon over the mushrooms and top with a handful of rocket or watercress.

5. Sprinkle with toasted pine nuts or sesame seeds and drizzle with olive oil, if desired. Serve straight away.

CARROT AND LENTIL SOUP

Vegan • **Serves:** 4–6 people • **Prep time:** 10 minutes
Cook time: 40 minutes

There are few things more comforting than a steaming bowl of homemade soup on a cold day (or when you are feeling under the weather). This is one of my favourites, as it is high in protein and fibre, thanks to the lentils, and can be made in bulk so that you have lunch prepared for the week ahead (it freezes beautifully too!). I like to serve with toasted sourdough or warm flatbread.

Benefits: Lentils are an excellent, affordable source of fibre, plant-based protein and iron. Plant-based iron absorption is enhanced with vitamin C, which can be found in sweet potatoes and carrots.

For the soup
1–2 tbsp olive oil
4 medium carrots, peeled and roughly chopped (weighing around 250g)
1 sweet potato, peeled and roughly chopped (weighing around 200g)
3 medium parsnips, peeled and roughly chopped (weighing about 500g)
1 red onion, roughly chopped
2 garlic cloves, grated
About 1 ½ tsp smoked paprika, to taste
400g tin of cooked (red) lentils, drained, or 100g dried
1.5l low or reduced salt vegetable stock
Salt and freshly ground black pepper, to taste

To serve
Toasted sourdough or warm flatbread
A sprinkling of toasted nuts or seeds for extra nutrients
  (optional)

1. Heat the oil in a large saucepan set over a medium heat. Add the carrots, sweet potato, parsnips and onion and cook for 8–10 minutes or until the onions are starting to soften.

2. Add the garlic and smoked paprika and cook for a further minute, stirring to coat the vegetables.

3. Pour in the vegetable stock and dried lentils, if using (if using tinned lentils, wait until the next step to add), and bring to the boil. Reduce the heat and simmer for 10 minutes.

4. Next, add the lentils if using cooked lentils (tinned, drained), then simmer for a further 20 minutes until thickened and all the vegetables have softened.

5. Season to taste and blitz using a handheld stick blender to your desired consistency.

6. Spoon into bowls and serve warm with your choice of bread.

Storage: Leave to cool completely before covering and chilling for up to three days in the fridge or keep for up to three months in the freezer.

MEDITERRANEAN MOZZARELLA, PESTO AND TOMATO WRAP

Vegetarian • **Makes:** 2 wraps • **Prep time:** 10 minutes
Cook time: 5 minutes (optional)

Wraps are one of my go-to lunch options, as they are perfect when I am working from home or out and about. This recipe is inspired by one of my favourite Italian salads, Insalata Caprese – with the addition of spinach for extra nutrients (you can also add cooked chicken, if desired). As always, I like to keep things flexible – you can swap the spinach for rocket or any other salad of your choice and use roasted vegetables instead of tomatoes, if you prefer. It is delicious served cold – but if you toast or griddle it in a dry pan, you get a slightly crisper exterior and wonderfully gooey mozzarella centre. Serve with a salad on the side for extra veggies, if you like.

Benefits: Wholewheat or seeded tortilla wraps are a good source of fibre, while tomatoes are an excellent source of lycopene, which is a powerful antioxidant. Mozzarella is a good source of protein and calcium – and is also lower in saturated fat than some other cheeses.

2 medium-sized wholewheat or seeded tortilla wraps
2–3 tbsp fresh pesto (see the recipe for my 'Pesto pasta Buddha bowl' on page 168 for my homemade pesto recipe)
2 small handfuls of fully prepared, washed and ready-to-eat spinach
1 ball of mozzarella, thoroughly drained and torn into pieces (125g drained weight)
12 cherry or baby plum tomatoes, halved
Freshly ground black pepper, to taste

1. Lay the tortilla wraps onto separate serving plates. Spread the pesto on top in an even layer.

2. Add a handful of spinach leaves to the middle of each wrap, taking care not to go too close to the edges. Scatter over the torn mozzarella pieces, top with the halved cherry or plum tomatoes and season with freshly ground black pepper, to taste. Flatten down the filling slightly.

3. Fold in the sides, bring up the bottom flap and tightly roll up towards the top, taking care to keep the filling enclosed and the sides folded in.

4. If serving cold, slice in half along the diagonal and serve straight away, or keep whole, put in an airtight container and chill in the fridge until ready to serve.

5. Alternatively, if you would like to serve hot, set a medium-sized non-stick frying pan over a low–medium heat. Add the unsliced wrap to the pan and dry fry for 2–3 minutes, pressing down with a spatula while it toasts, until the bottom is golden and crisp. Gently flip over and repeat on the other side. Remove from the pan, set onto a plate, slice in half on the diagonal and serve straight away.

Storage: Can be made up to step 4 up to 24 hours in advance and kept in an airtight container in the fridge. Slice in half just before serving.

TUNA NIÇOISE SALAD

Serves: 2 people • **Prep time:** 10 minutes
Cook time: 15 minutes

This simple salad is great to make when you have a busy day at home or want something to take with you on the go. I always have a couple of tins of sustainably sourced tuna (tinned in spring water, ideally) in my cupboard, as it is ideal for whipping up a nutritious meal in minutes. You can vary the salad leaves according to preference, choosing darker greens like spinach (which is higher in iron) if desired. This is very much a base recipe for you to customise according to your personal tastes – for example, you can add finely sliced red or spring onions, opt for green olives instead of black, or add non-traditional ingredients like sweetcorn to increase the veg.

Benefits: Eggs are a complete protein, which makes them a nutritional powerhouse – they provide multiple vitamins and minerals that support heart and brain health. Tuna is also an excellent, and affordable, protein. Where possible, always opt for sustainably sourced tuna, preferably tinned in water instead of brine or oil.

For the salad
Approximately 8–10 new potatoes
75g green beans, trimmed
3–4 eggs (depending on appetite)
2 little gem lettuces, trimmed and chopped
100g (approximately 7) cherry tomatoes or baby plum tomatoes, halved
50g fresh pitted black olives
160g can of tuna in olive oil or water, drained and broken into large chunks

For the dressing
(there will be some left over to use on your next salad)
4 tbsp extra virgin olive oil
1½ tbsp lemon juice
1 garlic clove, grated
1 tsp Dijon mustard
Salt and freshly ground black pepper, to taste

For the salad

1. Tip the uncooked new potatoes into a pan of cold, salted water, ensuring they're well covered. Bring to the boil, then reduce the heat to a simmer for 10–15 minutes until tender. Drain and leave to cool. Slice larger potatoes in half, if desired.

2. Meanwhile, blanch the green beans in boiling water until they are cooked to your liking. Drain them, then cool them quickly by rinsing them under cold water. Drain again and pat well with paper towel to dry the beans thoroughly.

3. Next, cook the eggs to your liking in a pan of simmering water. (For large eggs at room temperature: 6 minutes for soft boiled, 7 minutes for almost set, 8 minutes for softly set, 10 minutes for hard boiled. Adjust times as needed for medium eggs.) Drain the eggs, cool them in cold water and, when they are cool enough to handle, peel them. Set aside.

For the dressing

4. Place all the ingredients into a small jar, seal with a lid and shake well. Taste and adjust the seasoning as necessary.

To assemble the salad

5. Divide the little gem lettuce between 2 plates. Scatter the cherry or baby plum tomatoes, olives, green beans and potatoes on top, then add the tuna. Slice the eggs into halves (or quarters) and arrange on top.

6. Drizzle the dressing over the salad to taste, then serve.

Storage: Once dressed, this salad is best served straight away. If making ahead for lunch, leave salad undressed and store in an airtight container in the fridge. Enjoy within 24 hours, and add the dressing just before serving. Any leftover dressing will keep in the fridge for up to four days.

END OF WEEK 3 (LUNCH) REFLECTION

It's time to reflect on how the last week has gone. Pen to paper or in your mind, it's completely up to you, but the former is always preferable when it comes to reflecting on habit changes.

Reflection questions

Have a think about your answers to the following questions:

- **How did your new lunch choices impact your energy levels and overall mood?** Were there any changes?

- **Have you managed to consume fewer UPFs at your midday meal?** Think about the swaps that you have made.

- **Has including fewer UPFs and more whole foods made you feel better in the afternoon?** If the answer is yes, hopefully this highlights the benefits of choosing healthier, more wholefood and fewer ultra-processed alternatives. Consider the happiness and satisfaction that comes from consuming a meal you've made yourself. We value things more when we put the energy in, and cooking meals is no exception. You might find you are more mindful when eating home-cooked lunches, which will help to improve your digestion too.

- **Did you opt for a homemade sandwich over a shop-bought deal?** How much money would you save over the course of a month if you kept this up?

- **Did you find joy in making a nutrient-dense meal rather than settling for a convenient, UPF option?**

- **What practical shifts have you made to your daily routine?** Did you find it easy or a challenge to find time to prep more and get organised with your lunch options?

- **Do you feel less tempted to buy UPF sides, drinks or snacks if you have lunch with you?** What other positives are there? Have you reduced your sugar intake?

- **What did not go so well this week?** Reflecting on the barriers so you can learn and adapt is key for future success.

- **Were there days when you were busy or lacked ingredients, which made you choose a UPF lunch?** If so, did you choose a more or less nutritious option? How did you feel afterwards? It is not about feeling guilt or shame, but instead learning and making changes.

Remember, progress isn't linear, and there will be ups and downs along the way. Failure isn't about falling down, though, it's failing to get back up – this book will help you to get back up and realise that all is not lost. The 80/20 rule means that there *is* space for the occasional UPF – and ultimately, it's about cutting down, not out, for the majority of people.

If overall you are heading in the right direction (meaning you are consuming fewer UPFs generally) then hurray, you are a success! Just be persistent, consistent, resilient and believe in yourself.

> Consider finding someone who already has the healthy lunch habits that you would like and model them. 'You're the average of the five people you spend the most time with' is a quote attributed most often to motivational speaker Jim Rohn. Applying this to health, you could say that your health becomes the average of the five people who you spend the most time with.

Congratulations on completing week 3 – lunches! Are you ready for week 4, evening meals?

CHAPTER 8

WEEK 4 – EVENING MEALS

The evening meal, often referred to as dinner, supper or tea depending on where you're from, is one of the last opportunities to meet your five a day and 30g of fibre goal, and is the meal that will impact your sleep the most. The evening meal can also determine how successful the next day will be, depending on if you're cooking once and eating twice, or making time to prepare other meals as you cook.

A balanced evening meal can help to improve sleep quality through the provision of proteins and certain nutrients. This is because foods rich in tryptophan (lean meats, fish and tofu), magnesium (leafy greens, lentils, beans and seeds) and calcium (dairy, leafy greens and fish where you eat the bones, such as sardines) can help support muscle relaxation and the body's natural sleep-wake cycle (also known as the circadian rhythm).

Making sure that your evening meal doesn't leave you feeling uncomfortably full, and is eaten at least a couple of hours before bedtime, is important to allow adequate time for digestion to start and to prevent reflux (indigestion). Aim to include lean protein, wholegrains and at least two portions of vegetables, ideally with different colours to obtain a variety of different nutrients.

The evening is also a good opportunity to tune back into your physical body and the present moment, as the hustle and bustle of work or life admin and chores dies down. Eat slowly and notice when you are starting to feel full. It takes around 20 minutes for your brain to recognise that you're eating and for feelings of satiety to kick in.

Evening meals should ideally be eaten at a table, distraction free, and may also be a time to reconnect with friends and family. This tends to be more popular in countries such as Turkey, Italy, Spain and Greece versus the UK, where it is socially acceptable to eat in front of the TV. Studies show that if you are distracted when eating, you may eat more through the process of passive overconsumption (the overconsumption of calories without realising it).

NON-UPF VERSUS UPF EVENING MEAL OPTIONS

There's a wide spectrum of foods you can eat for an evening meal, and UPFs can be commonplace if time is of the essence – think ready meals, frozen pizzas and chips, instant noodles and even takeaways. Many typical takeaways, as well as fast food, contain highly processed ingredients and additives, as well as refined carbs and fried foods, which can be a source of trans fats (the worst type of fat for health).

Most ready meals are also classed as UPFs and can often be similar to takeaways, with low levels of vegetables and high amounts of saturated fat and refined carbs, as well as salt, additives and preservatives designed to enhance flavour, extend shelf life and improve convenience. If you do have a ready meal, choose one that contains lean protein such as beans or chicken, as well as a variety of vegetables (or add your own!) and, if possible, wholegrains like brown rice too. Let's take lasagne as an example. You could make it from scratch using lasagne sheets, passata from a jar or carton and cooked vegetables with lean mince, or you could buy a ready meal. The latter is certainly quicker, but will likely contain far less vegetables (to make it cheaper) and more in the way of salt and saturated fat. However, sometimes a ready meal is your only option and, in these instances, adding your own vegetables or salad as a side can be one way to increase fibre and nutritional value.

As discussed in previous chapters though, it's important not to demonise all UPFs, including ready meals and takeaways, as many can have their place from time to time, and are popular for bridging the gap between home-cooked food and convenience.

Red and processed meats feature a lot in the media, often scaring the public into thinking they should be avoided completely. It's true that high amounts are not encouraged, but they can still feature in a healthy and balanced diet, especially the fresh and lean varieties. The World Cancer Research Fund (WCRF) recommends no more than 350–500g of cooked red and processed meat a week (this equates to about 3 servings a week).

On the next page is a table showing the spectrum of non-UPF evening meals vs more- and less-nutritious UPF options.

Non-UPF evening meal examples	More-nutritious or less energy-dense UPF evening meal examples	Less-nutritious or more energy-dense UPF evening meal examples
Homemade pizza on a wholegrain wrap or pizza base (minimal additives, wholefood ingredients) with passata, two handfuls of chopped vegetables and freshly grated cheese	Supermarket fresh pizza – thin crust with chicken and vegetables, served with a green side salad	Supermarket frozen pizza topped with salami, served with (fried) French fries and tomato ketchup
Grilled salmon with paprika, served with brown rice and broccoli	Ready meal with brown rice, green vegetables, salmon and parsley sauce	Takeaway fish and chips with a side of bread and butter
Homemade vegetable stir fry with tofu and wholegrain noodles with a homemade sauce	Shop-bought sweet chilli sauce with pre-packed noodles, mixed vegetables and pre-cooked chicken	Instant noodle pot with chicken
Homemade bean burgers with (non-UPF) wholemeal baps and salad, with homemade sweet potato wedges	Supermarket bean burgers on a wholemeal bun with tomato ketchup and oven wedges	Ready to eat microwavable chicken burger with fries and sugary soda

HOW TO CHOOSE THE BEST OVEN PIZZA AND CHIPS

Pizza is often a go-to for many households, with some even making it a weekly ritual. I love this idea and would never suggest not doing it, however let's look at two packaged options and a homemade version to see what choices you could make in order to improve your nutritional intake and ultimately reduce your UPF consumption.

Evening meal 1 (less-nutritious UPF) – deep pan meat feast pizza, oven fries, tomato ketchup

Deep pan pizza ingredients – Wheat Flour, Water, Mozzarella Full Fat Soft Cheese (**Milk**) (13%), Smoked Pepperoni (6%) [Pork, Pork Fat, Salt, Dextrose, Antioxidants (Sodium Ascorbate, Ascorbic Acid, Extracts of Rosemary), Smoked Salt, Paprika Extract, White Pepper Extract, Preservative (Sodium Nitrite), Chilli Extract], Tomato Paste, Smoked Reformed Ham (3%) [Pork, Salt, Dextrose, Sugar, Stabilisers (Disodium Diphosphate, Pentasodium Triphosphate), Antioxidant (Sodium Ascorbate), Preservative (Sodium Nitrite)], Spicy Beef (3%) [Beef, Chilli], Yeast, Rapeseed Oil, Dextrose, Maize Starch, Salt, Basil, Sugar, Flavouring, Yeast Extract, Garlic Purée, Cayenne Pepper, Chilli, Garlic Powder, Cumin, Black Pepper, Coriander, Onion Powder, Cheese Powder (**Milk**), Paprika Extract, Oregano, Capsicum Extract, Flour Treatment Agent (Ascorbic Acid).

Contains 465 kcal (23%), 14.7g fat (21%), 6g saturates (30%), 5.4g sugars (6%), 1.8g salt (30%) per half a pizza.

Oven fries ingredients – Potato (92%), Sunflower Oil, Rice Flour, Potato Starch, Dextrin, Salt, Dextrose, Turmeric Powder.

Contains 259 kcal (13%), 7g fat (10%), 0.7g saturates (4%), 0.3g sugar (<1%), 0.52g salt (9%) per portion when cooked.

Tomato ketchup ingredients – *Tomato Purée, Sugar, Spirit Vinegar, Modified Maize Starch, Salt, Onion Powder, Flavouring, Garlic Powder, Spices.*

Contains 14 kcal, 0g fat, 2.8g sugar, 0.19g salt per tablespoon.

Evening meal 2 (more-nutritious UPF) – thin vegetable pizza, spicy potato wedges, low-sugar and -salt tomato ketchup

Thin pizza with vegetables ingredients – **Wheat** *Flour, Tomato Purée, Mozzarella Full Fat Soft Cheese (**Milk**) (7%), Marinated Grilled Red and Yellow Peppers (7%) [Red Pepper, Yellow Pepper, Sunflower Oil, Sugar, Salt, Concentrated Lemon Juice, Garlic, Chilli], Water, Cheddar Cheese (**Milk**) (5%), Red and Yellow Peppers (5%), Spinach (3.5%), Red Onion (3.5%), Spring Onion (2.5%), Onion, Emmental Medium Fat Hard Cheese (**Milk**), Single Cream (**Milk**), Crème Fraîche (**Milk**), Yeast, Dextrose, Rapeseed Oil, Salt, Blue Cheese (**Milk**), Sunflower Oil, Garlic, Sugar, Pea Starch, Dried Herbs, Spices, Potato Starch, Sourdough Culture (**Wheat**).*

Contains 350 kcal (18%), 10.7g fat (15%), 5.7g saturates (29%), 7g sugar (8%), 1.1g salt (18%) per half a pizza.

Spicy potato wedges ingredients – *Potato (93%), Sunflower Oil, Rice Flour, Salt, Potato Starch, Dextrin, Garlic Powder, Black Pepper, Red Pepper Flakes, Onion Powder, Flavouring, Chilli Powder.*

Contains 153 kcal (8%), 3.6g fat (5%), 0.4g saturates (2%), 0.5g sugar (1%), 0.41g salt (7%) per portion.

Low-sugar and -salt tomato ketchup ingredients – *Tomatoes (174g per 100g Tomato Ketchup), Spirit Vinegar, Sugar, Salt, Spice and Herb Extracts (contain Celery), Sweetener (Steviol Glycosides), Spice.*

Contains 10 kcal, 0g fat, 1.7g sugar, 0.14g salt per tablespoon.

Evening meal 3 (non-UPF) – homemade pizza, potato wedges and tomato ketchup

Homemade pizza ingredients – *Wholewheat pizza dough (for the base), tomato sauce (crushed tomatoes, garlic, herbs, salt, pepper), mozzarella cheese (milk), sliced bell peppers, onions, mushrooms, olives, cooked chicken breast.*

Potato wedges ingredients – *Potatoes, olive oil, paprika, garlic powder, salt, pepper.*

Homemade ketchup ingredients – *Crushed tomatoes, apple cider vinegar, honey, salt, onion powder, garlic powder.*

Or non-UPF ketchup ingredients – *Tomatoes (148g per 100g Tomato Ketchup), Spirit Vinegar, Sugar, Salt, Spice and Herb Extracts (contain Celery), Spice.*

As you could probably guess, the deep pan meat feast pizza is highest in calories, fat and salt, which together, when consumed in excess, can increase blood pressure and risks to heart health. The thinner, vegetable-based pizza has fewer calories and less fat along with more nutrients due to the vegetables, compared to the meat feast's offerings. Unsurprisingly, the homemade version is better in all categories, especially in the salt. The use of wholewheat dough and fresh veggies makes it an overall nutritious and well-balanced meal. To boost fibre and nutrient intake further, you could serve any of the pizza meal examples with a fresh salad – salad leaves, tomatoes, cucumber, red onion and avocado.

Now, let's turn our attention to another popular convenience meal – instant noodles! Both of the following examples are UPF foods, but comparing the two is helpful to empower you to make the choice that's right for you the next time you don't have time to make a dish from scratch.

Less-nutritious UPF noodles in a pot ingredients – *Noodle mix (95.3%): Dried noodles (64%) [***wheat*** flour (contains calcium carbonate, iron, niacin, thiamine), palm oil, salt, firming agents (potassium carbonates, sodium carbonates)],* ***wheat*** *flour, maltodextrin, flavour enhancers (monosodium glutamate, disodium guanylate, disodium inosinate), sugar, potato starch, lime juice powder (maltodextrin, lime juice), flavourings, potassium chloride, spices [cayenne pepper, garlic powder, smoked chilli powder], yeast extract, palm oil, onion powder, salt, red pepper, herbs (coriander leaves, oregano). Sauce sachet (4.7%): Chilli sauce (water, spirit vinegar, modified corn starch, salt, cumin, flavourings, cayenne pepper).*

More-nutritious UPF noodles in a ready meal ingredients – *Cooked rice noodles (29%) (rice flour, water, toasted* ***sesame seed*** *oil, rapeseed oil), water, soya strips (13%) (water, soya protein concentrate, sunflower oil, flavourings, dextrose, sugar, ginger purée, garlic purée, rice wine, cornflour, fermented* ***soya*** *bean, potato starch, toasted* ***sesame seed*** *oil, spices, rice vinegar, salt,* ***wheat*** *flour, colours (paprika extract, plain caramel), garlic, red rice koji,* ***sesame seed*** *oil), bean sprouts, carrot, red chilli, soybean curd (water,* ***soya*** *beans), spring greens, spring onion, rapeseed oil, garlic purée, ginger purée, sugar, spices, salt, cornflour, fermented soya bean,* ***wheat****, chopped coriander, concentrated* *vegetables (carrot, onion, leek), onion, **mustard** powder, dried red chilli, rice flour, sunflower oil.*

The differences between the UPF noodles in a pot and UPF noodles in a ready meal are quite significant. The first contains additives such as firming agents as well as flavour enhancers, is high in salt and lacks fibre. It also doesn't contain any vegetables. The second, however, contains protein, a mix of vegetables such as bean sprouts and carrots, as well as healthier fats like sesame seed oil, and spices for flavour. This noodle-based ready meal, although still high in salt, provides more fibre per serving and the inclusion of a variety of vegetables and plant-based proteins makes it a more balanced meal option, providing a range of nutrients and more satiety, too.

Both are convenient options, but the fresher ready meal is healthier from a nutrition point of view and contains fewer additives too.

WHAT ARE THE COMMON PROBLEMS WITH UPFs AT THE EVENING MEAL?

Have you ever eaten too many UPFs, or even sugar, and struggled to sleep? Some research has linked high-UPF diets with poorer quality sleep, with further suggestion that foods high in refined carbohydrates, in particular, can cause sharp rises in blood sugar, and subsequent lows, which can interrupt the body's natural calming-down process and cause restlessness, which can impact deep, restorative sleep.

To avoid experiencing issues with sleep caused by digestion, including reflux* (indigestion), plan to have balanced,

---

* Please speak to your GP if you continue to experience symptoms despite making dietary changes.

nutrient-dense evening meals that are cooked at home, at least a couple of hours before bedtime. Make sure to include plenty of vegetables, lean proteins such as chicken, fish, beans or another (non-UPF) plant-based alternative, and wholegrains, which will provide a steady release of energy and lead to better digestive health, increasing the chance of a better night's sleep. Try not to eat your evening meal too late – on evenings when you may be later home than usual, plan to have leftovers that can be reheated speedily, or defrost a pre-made meal to save time.

TOP TIPS FOR A HEALTHIER, LESS-PROCESSED EVENING MEAL

Here are my top tips to make your evening meal less about UPFs and a whole lot healthier as a result.

- **Make vegetables the stars of the plate:** having spoken to thousands of people over the years in my clinic, or at talks, it's apparent that for many, either the meat (protein) or potato (carb) part of the plate dominates, with vegetables often being an afterthought. Fresh and frozen vegetables (and salad) are not UPFs, and should be the stars of your evening meal. Aim for a couple of handfuls of vegetables at the least, for example, a handful of cauliflower and handful of broccoli, which provides two of your five a day, alongside salmon and brown rice.

- **Choose colour:** the more (natural) colours on your plate, the better. It indicates not only variety, which is key for a healthy gut microbiome (this may influence everything from immunity to mood), but a diverse range of phytochemicals (plant chemicals) as well as vitamins and minerals too.

- **Portioning your plate:** your chosen vegetables should cover around a third to half of your plate, then fill around a quarter to a third with protein (such as cod fillet, chicken or scrambled tofu) and the remaining quarter to a third with complex carbohydrates (such as wholegrains – think brown rice, quinoa or wholewheat pasta – or starchy vegetables [sweet potatoes or squash]). This balance helps to boost fullness as well as the fibre content of the meal, which helps to manage blood glucose levels too. (If you're especially active, you may require more carbohydrates.)

- **Accessorise with healthy fats:** fats are not to be feared, and when used in moderation they are a wonderful addition to the diet, from not only a taste but also a nutrient provision and vitamin absorption point of view too (vitamins A, D, E and K require fat to be absorbed by the body). Add around a tablespoon portion of healthy fats such as olive oil on a salad, or chopped or flaked nuts to a stir fry.

- **Choose healthier cooking methods:** opt for cooking methods that help to retain nutrients and don't use large amounts of oil (and always use fresh oil to prevent the formation of bad, trans fat), such as baking, steaming, poaching, microwaving (yes this is a great way of cooking vegetables!), air frying, slow cooking or grilling. These methods help preserve the vitamins and minerals in foods, while reducing the intake of any unhealthy fats. If you choose to use olive oil or rapeseed (vegetable) oil in cooking or meal prep, make sure to use the darker-coloured oils for salads and pasta dressings, and the more refined versions of olive or vegetable oils (more yellow in colour) for cooking at a high heat because they are more heat stable (and so won't smoke or go rancid).

- **Embrace wholegrains:** swap refined (or white) grains for wholegrains (usually brown in colour), which not only contain more fibre, but tend to have a lower glycaemic index (GI) too, which means a more gradual release in energy.

- **Make your own condiments:** while it may seem like a step too far for some, making your own condiments such as ketchup can put you in the driver's seat for better health. Condiments are often high in not only salt and sugar, but preservatives too.

- **Choose fewer-ingredient pre-prepared meals and add your own veg:** if you do choose to buy a ready meal, ignore any claims on the front and flip it over. Look at the ingredients list and choose those that are based on whole foods such as fish or beans, potatoes and vegetables with less additives such as emulsifiers and flavour enhancers. The shorter the ingredients list, the better in most cases. Add your own salad or vegetables for even more nutrients (cook frozen vegetables for speed).

- **Cook once, eat twice:** always plan to cook more than you need so you can have it for either lunch or dinner the following day, or freeze it for another day when you're short on time, instead of ordering a takeaway.

- **Prioritise meal planning your evening meal:** if I could choose only one mealtime to plan, it would be the evening meal as this is often cooked at home and for many, it's something to look forward to after a hard day at work or day doing chores. Have a go at planning your evening meals for the following week, and remember, it doesn't need to be a new meal every night of the week!

HEALTHY NON-UPF EVENING MEAL IDEAS

Here are ten dinner ideas using whole ingredients that you can enjoy throughout the week. Flick to the end of this chapter for five of my favourite healthy recipes, ideal for the evening meal.

1 **Mediterranean bean and vegetable stew:** one-pot meals are handy for reducing the amount of washing up. If you have a slow cooker, you could use that too. Stews are a great way of getting vegetables in, such as courgette, peppers, and tomatoes, and dried herbs like oregano. The beans act as a high-fibre, plant-based protein and the meal could be served with brown rice from the cupboard (I often choose microwavable bags for speed!).

2 **Lemon and garlic roasted chicken and vegetables:** this traybake idea involves roasting chicken with a variety of vegetables such as carrots, potatoes and peppers. A simple sauce of lemon juice, garlic and olive oil means none of the additives that are found in shop-bought marinades.

3 **Quinoa and black bean stuffed peppers:** fill bell peppers with a mixture of cooked quinoa (or rice), black beans, tinned sweetcorn, diced tomatoes and spices, then oven bake until the peppers are tender. Top with a sprinkle of cheese during the last few minutes of baking for a tasty finish.

4 **Sweet potato and chickpea curry:** a hearty and warming one-pot meal, this curry combines sweet potatoes and chickpeas in a coconut milk-based sauce with curry powder and other spices. With the right authentic recipes, it's easy to make your own curry sauce rather than buying a pre-made jar from the shop – or why not use a paste rather than a sauce as a stepping stone? You could also freeze this meal for the days when you don't have time to cook. Serve over brown

rice or with wholegrain naan plus a side of cooked spinach for a balanced meal.

5 **Baked salmon with asparagus and cherry tomatoes:** place salmon fillets on a baking sheet or in your air fryer alongside tenderstem broccoli, lemon slices and cherry tomatoes. Drizzle with a tablespoon of olive oil and season with salt and pepper. Bake until the salmon is flaky and the vegetables are cooked. Serve with homemade sweet potato wedges. We should aim to eat two portions of fish a week, one of which is oily for essential omega-3 fatty acids (if you don't eat fish, you may want to consider taking a supplement based on algae).

6 **Veggie-packed stir fry:** stir fry a variety of vegetables such as bell peppers, broccoli, sugar snap peas and carrots in a wok or large skillet. Add tofu or chicken for protein and toss everything with a sauce made from soy sauce, garlic and ginger. Serve over cooked wholegrain noodles. Yum.

7 **One-pan Greek-style chicken and orzo:** bake chicken breasts in a mixture of diced tomatoes, olives and orzo pasta, flavoured with garlic, lemon and oregano. The orzo cooks right in the pan, absorbing all the flavours.

8 **Ratatouille with jacket potato and cheese:** another classic way to get your vegetables in – try homemade ratatouille, or if you're short on time, tinned ratatouille for ease.

9 **Egg fried rice:** fancy a takeout but trying to cut down on your UPF intake? Choose wholegrain basmati rice in this healthier version of egg fried rice. Sauté the rice with peas, carrots, onions and scrambled eggs, then season with soy sauce and sesame oil for an easy and low-GI dinner option that won't leave you feeling bloated and sluggish.

10 **Sheet pan prawn fajitas:** toss prawns, sliced bell peppers and onions with a mix of fajita spices and olive oil. Spread on a baking sheet and roast until the prawns and veg are cooked. Serve with wholegrain tortillas and your favourite fajita toppings like guacamole and lime. Prawns are a wonderful lean protein to have instead of steak.

SHOPPING LIST EASY WINS – YOUR KITCHEN ESSENTIALS FOR A HEALTHIER EVENING MEAL

Some of these items may already be in your kitchen from previous weeks, and if so, they can be ticked off straight away.

Fresh produce and fridge items

- **Chicken or lean beef or a (non-UPF) vegetarian alternative**

- **Eggs or tofu**

- **Prawns, white fish or salmon**

- **Plain yoghurt and cheese**

- **Avocados**

- **Tomatoes, onions, mushrooms, green beans and peppers**

- **Lettuce and spinach**

Cupboard items

- **Brown basmati rice and brown pasta**, or couscous or quinoa if preferred.

- **Potatoes and sweet potatoes**

- **Tinned vegetables**, such as sweetcorn and peas.

- **Tinned fish in spring water or tomato sauce**, like tuna and mackerel.

- **Tinned beans**, like kidney beans and chickpeas.

- **Herbs and spices**

Frozen foods

- **Frozen vegetables**, such as sweetcorn, peas, edamame beans and spinach cubes.

- **Frozen fish**, for example plain white fish and prawns.

HOW TO ORGANISE YOUR KITCHEN FOR DINNER SUCCESS

You may have made some of the following changes already in the previous weeks, but if not, make them now in week 4.

- Use clear containers for your dry pasta, rice and other grains so that you can easily see what you have, and avoid buying duplicates.

- On your phone or in a physical format, make a list of healthy recipes that you enjoy and have them in a rota, categorised into seasons – for example, slow cooker dishes in autumn and winter, and salads in summer.

- Once a month declutter and clean the kitchen, including the fridge and freezer, to avoid having gone-off condiments hanging around for too long!

MEAL PLANNER WITH NON-UPF SNACKS, DRINKS, BREAKFASTS, LUNCHES AND EVENING MEALS

Energy levels and motivation in the evening may not be at the highest, and so the thought of cooking can be draining for some. Having a plan in place, though, can make cooking seem less daunting.

Top tip: if the dinner is freezable, like chickpea curry, I suggest you freeze a portion or two for the days where you really don't have the time or energy to cook from scratch. I can't stress this enough – cook once, eat twice!

	Monday	Tuesday	Wednesday
Breakfast	Overnight oats (see recipe on page 136) with nut butter and banana	Butterbean shakshuka (see recipe on page 141)	Vegan oaty blueberry muffins (see recipe on page 134)
Morning snack	Apple and cheese	Oatcakes topped with nut butter and banana slices	Berries with plain yoghurt and a drizzle of honey if desired
Lunch	Pesto pasta Buddha bowl (see recipe on page 168)	Smahed avocado, feta and eggs on wholegrain bread (see recipe on page 174)	Tuna niçoise salad (see recipe on page 181)
Afternoon snack	Carrots and hummus – homemade (see recipe on page 85) or shop bought	Dark chocolate and coconut energy balls (see recipe on page 88)	Small bag of popcorn – or pop at home with kernels
Evening meal	Paneer curry (see recipe on page 219)	Herby cod with crispy potato traybake (see recipe on page 210)	Mixed bean chilli (see recipe on page 213)
Dessert/ evening snack			
Drinks	Water and warm golden milk with turmeric	Water and hot chocolate made from warm milk, cocoa powder and a dash of maple syrup	Water and strawberry- and cucumber- infused water

Week 4 – evening meals

Thursday	Friday	Saturday	Sunday
Peanut butter and banana on wholegrain toast	Greek yoghurt pancakes (see recipe on page 132)	Sweet potato fritters (see recipe on page 139)	Spinach and mushroom omelette
Healthy trail mix – made from plain nuts, dried fruit and dark chocolate	Dried apricots and almonds	Medjool dates stuffed with nut butter and a little dark chocolate	Avocado on a wholegrain cracker with slices of boiled egg
Mediterranean mozzarella, pesto and tomato wrap (see recipe on page 179)	Carrot and lentil soup (see recipe on page 177)	Hummus with garlic and herb mushrooms on sourdough toast (see recipe on page 175)	Sunday dinner with all the trimmings
Roasted butter beans with olive oil and spices	No-bake fruit and oat bars (see recipe on page 90)	Pear and a handful of walnuts	Roasted kale crisps
Baked salmon with crunchy crispbread topping and sweet potato wedges (see recipe on page 208)	Vegetable noodle stir fry (see recipe on page 216)	Chicken fajitas with wholegrain wraps	Loaded jacket potatoes
Water and herbal tea of choice	Water and lemon, ginger and honey tea (see recipe on page 107)	Water and fresh carrot and orange juice (see recipe on page 105)	Water and date, banana and cocoa smoothie (see recipe on page 104)

YOUR FIVE-STEP HEALTHY CHECKLIST FOR WEEK 4 (EVENING MEAL)

As we started in week 1, take a look at the goals that follow and choose which of them you want to work on.

Tick on the left if you want to work on a particular goal, and on the right when you have achieved it:

Tick to work on ✔	Goal	Tick when completed ✔
	Pick your favourite takeaway dish and make a healthier version of it – for example, homemade pizzas loaded with vegetables or a chicken curry.	
	Use your plate as a guide for balance. Fill: • a quarter to a third (or more if needed) of the plate with starchy carbohydrates such as potato or rice (preferably wholegrain) • a quarter to a third (or more if needed) of the plate with protein like salmon, tofu or chicken • a third to half of the plate with salad or vegetables such as broccoli and carrots.	
	If you do have a ready meal at home, add a serving of vegetables or salad to it.	
	Use a healthier cooking method such as steaming, microwaving or air frying	
	Plan your evening meals for the week ahead, trying just one new recipe and making sure to cook once and eat twice (make more than what you need, at least one night of the week).	

NON-UPF HEALTHY EVENING MEAL RECIPES

Before we move on to our weekly reflection and bonus week of desserts (which hopefully will feel like the easiest week as it is totally optional!), here are five of my favourite non-UPF healthy evening meal recipes. Choose one or two and give them a go.

- Baked salmon with crunchy crispbread topping and sweet potato wedges

- Herby cod with crispy potato traybake

- Mixed bean chilli

- Vegetable noodle stir fry

- Paneer curry

BAKED SALMON WITH CRUNCHY CRISPBREAD TOPPING AND SWEET POTATO WEDGES

Serves: 2 people • **Prep time:** 5 minutes
Cook time: 30 minutes

I have been making this recipe for years, thanks to my mum, as it is simple to make, delicious and packed full of nutrients (and is the perfect way to get even fish-avoiders to enjoy eating fish!). You only need a handful of ingredients, and the prep is minimal – making it ideal for those busy weeknights when you are low on energy and time, but still want to enjoy a nourishing meal. While this recipe includes tenderstem broccoli, I like to vary the greens according to what is in season – green beans, asparagus, spinach and cavolo nero all work well too. Choose sustainably sourced salmon so that it's not only great for your health, but good for the ocean too.

Benefits: Salmon is an excellent source of protein and omega-3 fatty acids, and counts as one of the two recommended portions of fish we should be eating every week to support our heart and brain health.

3 seeded rye crispbreads, crushed (using a pestle and mortar or a rolling pin)
Handful of fresh coriander or parsley, roughly chopped, or homemade pesto (see the recipe for my 'Pesto pasta Buddha bowl' in Chapter 7 [Week 3 – lunches] for my homemade pesto recipe)
Olive oil, for drizzling
Salt and freshly ground black pepper, to taste
2 salmon fillets

Approximately 6 heaped tbsp Greek yoghurt
2 medium-sized sweet potatoes, scrubbed and cut into
  wedges
Dried mixed herbs, to taste
2 handfuls (approximately 160g) of tenderstem broccoli

1. Preheat the oven to 200°C/180°C fan.

2. Add the crushed rye crispbreads to a bowl, along with the fresh coriander (or parsley or homemade pesto), a drizzle of olive oil and seasoning, to taste, before mixing together. Set to one side.

3. Place the salmon fillets (skin side down if they have skin) on a non-stick baking sheet and spread the yoghurt over the top of each fillet. Sprinkle over the rye crispbread mix and press down gently.

4. On a separate baking sheet, lay the potato wedges in a single layer, drizzle with olive oil and season with salt and dried mixed herbs. Toss gently to coat.

5. Place the sweet potatoes in the oven and roast for 10 minutes before adding the salmon on a separate shelf and cooking both trays for a further 20 minutes, turning the sweet potato wedges half-way through cooking, until they are crispy and the salmon is just cooked (the exact time will depend on the size and thickness of the salmon fillets).

6. During the last 5 minutes of cooking time, steam or lightly boil the tenderstem broccoli.

7. Place the salmon onto a serving plate and serve with the sweet potato wedges and tenderstem broccoli.

Storage: This meal is best served straight away. Any leftover salmon can be cooled completely before being covered and chilled for up to three days.

HERBY COD WITH CRISPY POTATO TRAYBAKE

Serves: 4 people • **Prep time:** 10 minutes
Cook time: 45 minutes

This veg-packed, Mediterranean-style traybake is ideal for a nutritious mid-week dinner, as it has minimal prep and minimal washing up! Like most of my recipes, it is incredibly versatile. You can swap the cod for another white fish such as hake, or you can use salmon, for one of your weekly portions of oily fish (always choose sustainably sourced fish where possible). Chicken breasts also work well, but remember to adjust the cooking time accordingly (they will need about 25 minutes to cook, depending on the size, or you can cook them until the juices run clear).

This traybake can be easily adapted to accommodate what's already in your fridge. For example, add sliced courgettes with the peppers, or a handful of olives with the cherry tomatoes (bear in mind that olives will be salty, so hold back on the seasoning elsewhere if you do use them).

Benefits: The Mediterranean diet is one of the healthiest on the planet. It is rich in unsaturated fats from nuts and olive oil, and leans heavily on fresh, seasonable vegetables, fruits, herbs, wholegrains and lean proteins.

For the traybake
750g baby new potatoes
3 tbsp olive oil
1 unwaxed lemon – zest and juice
10g thyme, fresh leaves picked and finely chopped,
*   or 2 tsp dried mixed herbs*
Salt and freshly ground black pepper, to taste

2 red, yellow or orange peppers, deseeded and sliced into wedges

2 red onions, peeled and quartered (cut into eights for large onions)

4 cod fillets or loins (weighing about 170g each)

6 cloves of garlic, peeled

400g cherry tomatoes or baby plum tomatoes

To serve

Fresh pesto to drizzle (optional) – see the recipe for my 'Pesto pasta Buddha bowl' in Chapter 7 (Week 3 – lunches) for my homemade pesto recipe

Freshly chopped parsley or fresh basil leaves

1. Preheat the oven to 200°C/180°C fan.

2. In a large bowl, toss the baby new potatoes with 2 table-spoons of the olive oil, the zest of 1 lemon, thyme (or mixed herbs) and salt and pepper. Tip onto a large baking sheet and spread in a single layer. Roast in the oven for 15 minutes.

3. Meanwhile, in the same bowl used for the potatoes, combine the onions and peppers with the remaining 1 tablespoon of oil. Season with salt and freshly ground black pepper and mix well.

4. Remove the baking sheet from the oven, add the vegetables to it and mix everything well. Return the tray to the oven for another 15 minutes.

5. In the meantime, check the cod for any bones before squeezing the juice from the lemon over the fish.

6. Remove the tray from the oven, scatter over the garlic and cherry tomatoes and mix well so that everything is evenly distributed across the tray. At this point, you should also turn the potatoes, peppers and onions to ensure even cooking.

Nestle the cod fillets (or loins) amongst the vegetables, ensuring the cod portions are spaced well apart from each other, then return the baking tray to the oven for another 12–15 minutes, or until the cod is cooked and flakes easily with a fork (the exact time needed will depend on the size, shape and thickness of your cod, take care to ensure it doesn't over-cook) and the vegetables are tender and lightly caramelised.

7. Spoon onto serving plates, drizzle with fresh pesto and garnish with freshly chopped parsley or fresh basil leaves.

Storage: This dish is best enjoyed right after cooking, but left-overs can be left to cool before covering and chilling in the fridge for up to three days.

MIXED BEAN CHILLI

Vegan • **Serves:** 4 people • **Prep time:** 10 minutes
Cook time: 20–25 minutes

This mixed bean chilli is both nutritious and delicious. It is also ideal for batch-cooking and it never gets dull, as you can mix and match how you serve it – pop it into tortilla wraps and serve with my simple smashed avocado and homemade salsa, enjoy it as a jacket potato filling with grated cheese, serve with homemade baked potato wedges or steamed rice – all finished off with your choice of herbs and wedges of lime for a refreshing zing. This recipe is full of flavour, but is still fairly mild, so adjust the heat accordingly if you prefer something a little spicier.

Benefits: The high fibre content in beans and vegetables like onions, peppers and tomatoes promotes healthy digestion. Avocados are an excellent source of healthy monounsaturated fats and vitamin E.

For the chilli
1–2 tbsp olive oil
1 onion, finely chopped
1 red, yellow or orange pepper, halved, deseeded and
  chopped
3 garlic cloves, crushed
2 tsp smoked paprika
1 tsp mild chilli powder, or to taste
2 tsp ground cumin
1 tsp dried oregano
1 tbsp tomato purée
1 tsp unsweetened cocoa powder
400g tin chopped tomatoes

400g tin mixed beans, drained and rinsed
400g tin black beans, drained and rinsed
Salt, to taste

For the smashed avocado
2 medium-sized ripe avocados, peeled, stones removed,
* and sliced*
2 cloves garlic, crushed
1 tbsp freshly chopped coriander (optional)
Lime juice, to taste
Pinch of chilli flakes, to taste (optional)
Salt, to taste

To serve
Jacket potatoes, homemade baked potato wedges or
* brown rice*
Freshly chopped coriander or finely chopped chives
Sliced spring onions
Plain yoghurt of your choice (optional)
Grated cheese or vegan-friendly alternative (optional)
Lime wedges (optional)

1. Heat the oil in a medium-sized hob-safe casserole dish set over a medium heat, and fry the onion and pepper for 10 minutes, stirring often, until golden and starting to soften.

2. Add the garlic, smoked paprika, mild chilli powder, dried cumin, dried oregano, tomato purée and cocoa powder and continue to cook for 1 minute, stirring often.

3. Pour in the chopped tomatoes, mixed beans and black beans. Rinse out the tin of tomatoes with 100ml water and add to the pan. Add a pinch of salt, stir and bring to a simmer.

4. Moderate the heat and simmer for 20–25 minutes, stirring occasionally, until thickened.

5. Meanwhile, make the smashed avocado: tip the avocados into a bowl and mash with a fork to break down to the consistency you desire (depending on whether you prefer it chunky or smooth). Mix in the garlic, coriander (if using) and lime juice, chilli flakes and salt, to taste. Set aside.

6. Once the chilli has thickened and reduced, taste and adjust the seasoning and spices to suit your preference. Serve warm with your choice of either jacket potatoes, homemade baked potato wedges or rice, with a spoonful of the smashed avocado. Garnish with your choice of toppings – I like to mix it up each time, but my favourites include: freshly chopped coriander, finely chopped chives, sliced spring onions, a spoonful of plain yoghurt, grated cheese and lime wedges.

Storage: Serve straight away or leave to cool completely before storing in an airtight container in the fridge for up to three days. The smashed avocado will also keep for up to three days in an airtight container, but will lose its vivid green colour and will start to go brown – adding an avocado stone to the centre of the container will help slow down this process.

VEGETABLE NOODLE STIR FRY

Adaptable for vegetarians and vegans
Serves: 2 people • **Prep time:** 5 minutes
Cook time: 15–20 minutes

Stir fries are a brilliant way to make a nutritious meal in a matter of minutes. They are incredibly versatile and can be easily adjusted to suit the ingredients you already have at home, or adapted to accommodate numerous dietary requirements. I have included a suggestion for leftover roast chicken in this recipe, but you could omit the meat to keep this vegan-friendly, and instead opt for a plant-based protein like tofu. Equally, you can switch up the veggies for baby corn, mushrooms, mange-tout or beansprouts, as well as try different noodles (egg, rice, udon, etc). I have included various suggestions for toppings to help make it family-friendly (not everyone likes chilli) and to encourage diversity. Get imaginative and create your very own signature stir fry!

Benefits: Wholewheat noodles are a good source of fibre, while peppers are high in vitamin C to help support the immune system. Sesame seeds are a great way to add extra fibre, protein and healthy fats to meals.

For the homemade stir fry sauce (this will make extra)
5 tbsp low-salt soy sauce
1 tbsp toasted sesame oil
1 unwaxed lemon – zest and juice
2 tbsp runny honey, or maple syrup for a vegan option
1 tsp garlic paste
2 tsp ginger paste
½ tsp Chinese five spice or a pinch of dried chilli flakes

For the noodles

2 nests of dried wholewheat noodles (weighing about 130g)
100g edamame beans
2 spring onions, thinly sliced
1 carrot, grated
1 tbsp sesame oil

For the stir fry

1–2 tbsp vegetable oil
1 red, yellow or orange pepper, halved, deseeded and thinly
   sliced
80g sugar snap peas, halved lengthways
About 3 tbsp homemade stir fry sauce
About 140g cooked chicken or tofu (optional)
1–2 tbsp water, if needed

To serve

Sesame seeds
Peanuts or cashew nuts (optional)
1 red chilli, thinly sliced (optional)
Spring onions, thinly sliced
Freshly chopped coriander

For the homemade stir fry sauce

1. Whisk together all ingredients for the sauce in a small bowl,
    then set aside.

For the noodles

2. Cook the noodles with the edamame beans according to
    the packet instructions, drain well, rinse under cold water,
    drain again and tip into a bowl with the sliced spring onion
    and grated carrot. Drizzle with the sesame oil, toss well and
    set aside.

For the stir fry

3. Set a medium-sized frying pan with the vegetable oil over a medium heat.

4. When hot, add the peppers and sugar snap peas to the pan, and cook for 5–7 minutes or until the veggies start to soften.

5. Add the stir fry sauce and stir to coat the vegetables.

6. Remove from the heat and tip in the noodles and chicken or tofu (if using). Toss gently with the vegetables to coat, adding a splash of water, if needed, to loosen.

7. Return the pan to the heat and gently toss the contents for 1–2 minutes to heat through the noodles and chicken.

8. Divide between 2 bowls, sprinkle with sesame seeds, your choice of nuts, sliced chilli (if desired), spring onions and freshly chopped coriander and serve immediately.

Storage: This dish is best served straight away. The sauce can be made in advance and kept in a sealed airtight jar or small container in the fridge for up to five days.

PANEER CURRY

Vegetarian • **Serves:** 4 people • **Prep time:** 10 minutes
Cook time: 40 minutes

This is a classic fakeaway option – and a healthy twist on one of my favourite takeaway dishes. If you've never tried paneer before, it's very similar to a halloumi cheese (which also works well in this dish), and has a mild taste and soft-medium texture – making it perfect to add to a curry. If you do eat meat, you can use diced chicken breast instead of paneer, but always check to ensure it is cooked through before serving.

Benefits: Paneer is an excellent source of protein and calcium, which is needed for repairing and building muscles – and maintaining healthy bones.

For the curry
1 tbsp olive oil
1 brown onion, diced
2 cloves garlic, diced
2 bell peppers, chopped
200g paneer cheese, chopped into chunks
1 tbsp mild curry powder, or to taste
1½ tsp ground turmeric
1 tsp ground cumin
½ tsp chilli flakes, or to taste
400g tin coconut milk
400g tin chopped tomatoes
200g frozen peas or spinach

To serve
Swirl of yoghurt (optional)
Freshly chopped coriander (optional)

Toasted cashew nuts, flaked almonds or coconut flakes (optional)
Rice or flatbread

1. Heat a wide pan on a medium heat and add the olive oil and the onion to soften for 3–4 minutes.

2. Add the garlic, pepper, paneer and spices. Fry on a medium heat for approximately 5 minutes, stirring to coat the paneer and peppers with the spices.

3. Add the tinned coconut milk and chopped tomatoes, stir to combine and simmer for around 20 to 30 minutes on a low to medium heat to allow the liquid to reduce.

4. Stir in the frozen peas or spinach and cook for a further 5 minutes or until defrosted and heated through.

5. Serve warm with a sprinkle of coriander, a dollop of yoghurt, if desired, toasted nuts if desired, and rice or a side of your choice!

Storage: This dish is best enjoyed immediately, but can be left to cool completely before being covered and chilled in the fridge for up to three days.

END OF WEEK 4 (EVENING MEAL) REFLECTION

Grab a drink and let's reflect on week 4 with our evening meals.

Reflection questions

Have a think about your answers to the following questions:

- **Did your dinner plate composition start to change at all?** Perhaps you added more vegetables, or were more mindful about the amount of fat being used in cooking.

- **Did you try any new healthier cooking methods such as microwaving, air frying or steaming?** You may have also used a slow cooker.

- **Did you find yourself using new spices that you forgot you had since clearing out your cupboards?** How did that impact the amount of salt being used (hopefully you will have used less!).

- **Did you find the time to cook at least one evening meal from scratch (using no UPFs)?** How did it feel?

- **Did you try one healthy new, non-UPF recipe?** How did it go?

- **Have you noticed any changes in digestion, energy or even sleep?**

- **Do you like leftovers and eating the same meal again or do you need variety and prefer to freeze meals for future weeks instead?** Adjust your meal plan accordingly for next week.

- **Did you mindlessly snack or graze while cooking?** If you did, how could you reduce this the next time you cook? Could you have a glass of water instead?

Based on this week's reflections, identify one or two aspects of your dinner routine you'd like to continue improving or experimenting with. Maybe it's exploring more plant-based recipes, continuing to reduce UPF consumption or getting more experimental with leftovers.

We've now come to the end of your four-week plan to reduce the number of UPFs you're eating, but I've included a bonus week 5 to cover desserts (in case you're partial!). If you don't have a sweet tooth, you can skip to the conclusion part of the book on page 245! Well done on getting this far!

This book isn't designed to be read from cover to cover and then to be put down and forgotten about. It's a book that I encourage you to refer to if you have questions, or if you need inspiration for a particular meal time. It's a book that will stay with you throughout your journey to reducing your UPFs, one meal at a time.

CHAPTER 9

(BONUS)
WEEK 5 – DESSERTS

Dessert is often the course of a meal that is most looked forward to, with many of us feeling like we have a separate stomach made especially for it! Desserts are sadly a prime category for UPFs and can be high in both sugar and fat – take the classic microwavable sticky toffee pudding for example (delicious, yet still a UPF sadly). You might be thinking, how on earth am I expected to eat desserts without consuming UPFs? Well, with the 80/20 rule that we touched on earlier in this book, it is possible to enjoy desserts in moderation and still be healthy, UPF or not. Read on to find out how to have your cake and eat it too.

As a reminder, the 80/20 rule is a guideline that encompasses eating healthy and nutrient-dense foods (i.e. whole foods) around 80 per cent of the time (i.e. the majority of the time), and less nutrient-dense foods (or UPFs high in salt, sugar and fat) around 20 per cent of the time. Within a healthy and balanced diet, we can still enjoy our favourite desserts that provide minimal nutritional value without guilt and without derailing our nutritional goals. This is because food is not just for fuel, it is for enjoyment too.

HOW MUCH IS TOO MUCH?

If you like to enjoy something sweet after a meal then you're not alone, but *what* you have will dictate how much your dietary intake needs to change. Fruit and plain yoghurt, for example, even with a drizzle of honey, is a highly nutritious non-UPF dessert, and is in a completely different league to those UPF gooey pots of chocolatey and caramel deliciousness that you can buy. If UPF desserts such as these are creeping into your diet on an almost daily basis then there may be a few swaps to be made, as we will discuss. If you simply enjoy them occasionally, then go easy on yourself – a little bit of what you fancy does you good, after all.

One habit that you could add to your week is to look at the week ahead and see where you are going to be consuming (or would like to be consuming!) UPF desserts – for example, at a birthday party or even a movie night – then plan those desserts in, and enjoy them! In the days before and after, you could plan to eat fewer (less-nutritious) UPFs than usual.

So, the next time you're planning your weekly meals and find yourself pondering about dessert, remember that it's not just about cutting out UPFs entirely, but instead making smarter choices most of the time. This way, when you do decide to have that piece of cake or a scoop or two of ice cream, it becomes a mindful choice rather than a mindless act of eating. Desserts are a pleasure to be enjoyed, and there's no need to cut them out altogether.

NON-UPF VERSUS MORE- AND LESS-NUTRITIOUS UPF DESSERTS

When it comes to desserts, there is no shortage of options and often a full aisle's worth is dedicated to them in the supermarket. From ice cream to microwavable puddings, the variety and availability of ultra-processed options can feel endless. Let's consider the example of a chocolate dessert, everyone's favourite, in three different forms: a ready-made (high in sugar and fat) chocolate dessert pot, a lighter chocolate mousse, and Greek yoghurt mixed with cocoa powder and a touch of honey – the key is to make an informed decision as to what you want, when.

Here are a few more examples:

Non-UPF dessert examples	More-nutritious or less energy-dense UPF dessert examples	Less-nutritious or more energy-dense UPF dessert examples
Greek yoghurt mixed with cocoa powder and a little honey – topped with crushed nuts	Lighter chocolate mousse – shop bought	Gooey chocolate dessert pots – shop bought
Homemade healthier rocky road*	Raisin and oat cookies – shop bought	Double chocolate chip cookies – shop bought
Homemade pear and almond traybake*	Lower-sugar fruit sorbet – shop bought	Chocolate ice cream – shop bought
Homemade cherry crumble*	Milky puddings, e.g. rice pudding or custard with fruit	Chocolate cake – shop bought

HOW TO CHOOSE BETWEEN TWO UPF DESSERTS

Let's look at the nutritional difference between two of the UPF chocolate dessert examples listed in the table.

Less-nutritious UPF gooey chocolate mousse and ganache ingredients *– Milk Chocolate (40%) (Sugar, Cocoa Butter,*

---

* *The recipes for these options can be found at the end of this chapter!*

*Whole **Milk** Powder, Cocoa Mass, Emulsifier (Soya Lecithin), Natural Flavouring), Whipping Cream (**Milk**), Pasteurised **Egg** White, Pasteurised **Egg** Yolk, Salted Butter (Butter (**Milk**), Salt), Whole **Milk**, Dark Chocolate (6%) (Cocoa Mass, Sugar, Fat Reduced Cocoa Powder, Emulsifier (**Soya** Lecithin)), Sugar, Glucose Syrup, Stabilisers (Guar Gum, Xanthan Gum), Preservative (Potassium Sorbate), Fat Reduced Cocoa Powder, Acidity Regulator (Citric Acid), Water.*

More-nutritious and less energy-dense UPF lighter milk chocolate dessert ingredients *– Water, Skimmed **Milk** from Concentrate, Belgian Milk Chocolate (6%) (Sugar, Cocoa Butter, Whole **Milk** Powder, Cocoa Mass, Emulsifier **Soya** Lecithin; Natural Vanilla Flavouring), Sugar, Modified Maize Starch, Fat Reduced Cocoa Powder, Cream (**Milk**), Stabilisers: Pectins, Carob Bean Gum, Sweeteners: Aspartame, Acesulfame K, Flavourings.*

The gooey dessert contains ingredients such as milk chocolate, whipping cream, salted butter and dark chocolate, which are all high in saturated fat. However, it also includes stabilisers and preservatives like guar gum, xanthan gum and potassium sorbate, which are common in UPFs to maintain texture and extend shelf life. A single pot packs 20g of fat and 18g of sugar, which is a lot to take in from one relatively small dessert.

The lighter milk chocolate dessert uses water and skimmed milk from concentrate as its base, lowering the calorie content. It's thickened with modified maize starch (making it a UPF still), and has added cream, but has a lower fat content at under 3g. It contains stabilisers such as pectins and carob bean gum as well as the artificial sweeteners aspartame and acesulfame K, reducing its sugar content to 9.6g of sugar per pot.

I'm not saying for a minute that one of these pots is 'better' than the other, however given that both are UPFs, if you get a similar level of satisfaction from both, then it may be advantageous to choose the one that provides less sugar and fat, depending on how often you are consuming it. Making your own non-UPF dessert at home though *is* obviously better than both of the UPF examples!

A great example of a non-UPF chocolate dessert would be Greek yoghurt mixed with cocoa powder and a little honey. This is a more nutritious, yet still speedy, homemade dessert option. The yoghurt contains probiotics, which are beneficial for gut health, and it contains protein and calcium too. Cocoa powder adds a deep chocolate flavour without the added sugars and fats found in chocolate bars, while the honey brings a natural sweetness that can be easily controlled from a quantity point of view. Add a handful of berries for a fibre and nutrient boost, too.

WHAT ARE THE COMMON ISSUES WITH HAVING (TOO MANY) UPF DESSERTS?

Most UPF desserts are what we call 'fun foods' as they provide little in the way of vitamins and fibre, yet they taste delicious. Fun foods such as these could cause an excess in calorie consumption* if consumed frequently, but are fine to be eaten occasionally within the context of a healthy and balanced diet.

Choosing to have non-UPF desserts that are made at home more often is always going to be more beneficial to our health, as it gives us more choice around what ingredients we use, and we can strike a balance between deliciousness and health.

TOP TIPS FOR HEALTHIER, LESS-PROCESSED DESSERTS

If you want to decrease the amount of UPF desserts you are consuming, consider the following tips:

---

* Everyone has their own unique energy requirements based on genetics, build (including body composition), age, lifestyle and activity levels.

- **Homemade over shop-bought:** when possible, make your own desserts. This allows you to choose the ingredients, meaning you can experiment with using natural sugars or use less of them.

- **Consider portion size:** if you choose a ready-made dessert, have a smaller portion and have it with a handful or two of your favourite fruits or high-protein plain yoghurt instead of cream.

- **Focus on quality, not quantity:** enjoying a smaller amount of a rich, satisfying dessert, such as one macaroon, may be more satisfying than a bigger portion of lighter mousse, for example. Portion size matters, and only you know how you respond to different foods.

- **Incorporate fruits:** fruits can be a sweet, natural base for desserts, meaning you can reduce any added sugar. Think baked pears, stewed berries or mixed chopped fruit. A personal favourite of mine is Medjool dates stuffed with nut butter topped or coated with dark chocolate and a little sea salt for flavour – delicious!

- **Choose dark chocolate:** for chocolate cravings, dark chocolate with a high cocoa content (70 per cent or above) is a lower-sugar, healthier choice. It's also a lot harder to overeat due to the richness in flavour.

- **Experiment with sweetness:** explore natural sweeteners such as honey, maple syrup, mashed banana or dates to add sweetness to desserts without using more refined sugars. For example, mashed banana is a good binder and a sweet addition to muffins.

- **Nutrient-dense additions:** incorporate nuts, seeds or wholegrains to add texture, fibre and nutrients to desserts

– for example, add ground almonds to carrot cake and use wholemeal flour in cakes.

- **Practise mindful eating:** don't eat your dessert while doing or watching something else, enjoy every bite and savour it to feel more satisfied once it's gone!

- **Think outside the box:** chocolate-based breakfast cereals and snack bars are still UPFs, but they are often more nutritious and may provide less sugar and more fibre than typical chocolate-based desserts.

- **Try a herbal drink:** if you want to cut down on the amount of desserts you are having, some people find that a warm drink after a meal can help to curb sweet cravings. Try peppermint or even liquorice tea.

HEALTHY NON-UPF DESSERT IDEAS

Here are five healthier non-UPF dessert ideas using whole ingredients that you can enjoy throughout the week. Flick to the end of this chapter for four of my favourite healthy recipes (including a five-minute mug cake that I just *had* to include!).

1 **Greek yoghurt topped with fruits of choice, a little honey and nuts:** flaked almonds or crushed walnuts work well and provide healthy fats as well as crunch. If you're out of yoghurt, try blending frozen banana to make a deliciously creamy plant-based dessert, ready to be topped with chocolate chips (my choice!) and chopped hazelnuts.

2 **Medjool dates stuffed with nut butter, topped or coated in melted dark chocolate:** leave these to set in the fridge and enjoy when you fancy something sweet.

3 **Homemade healthier hot chocolate:** simply add cocoa powder along with your chosen sweetener to your preferred warm milk.

4 **Chocolate peanut butter bark:** a three-ingredient frozen snack! All you need is a banana sliced onto greaseproof paper, smooth over your choice of nut butter and then drizzle melted chocolate over to create a three-tier bark. Once frozen it's great for snapping off chunks when you're feeling peckish, or for enjoying over yoghurt.

5 **Five-minute chocolate orange mug cake:** mug cakes are such a life saver for when you have cravings but don't have any comforting snacks in! The beauty of this recipe is that it contains a lot less sugar than normal mug cakes but still is delicious – see the recipe at the end of this chapter.

SHOPPING LIST EASY WINS – YOUR KITCHEN ESSENTIALS FOR HEALTHIER DESSERTS

Some of these items may already be in your kitchen from previous weeks and, if so, they can be ticked off straight away.

Fresh produce and fridge items

- **Bananas and fresh berries**

- **Carrots**, grated for carrot cake muffins.

- **Eggs**, or replacements for baking, such as chia seeds or flaxseeds.*

- **Dairy or plant-based milk**, ideally fortified with calcium.

- **Plain yoghurt, Greek yoghurt**

---

* To replace one egg in most recipes, mix 1 tablespoon of flaxseeds with 3 tablespoons of water and leave to stand for five minutes to thicken.

Cupboard items

- **Oats and wholemeal flour**, for baking.

- **Dried fruit**, like Medjool dates and apricots.

- **Nuts and seeds**, including ground almonds and chia seeds.

- **Nut butters**, such as almond, cashew or peanut butter.

- **Tinned fruit**, such as pears in juice not syrup.

- **Ground cinnamon**, or ginger.

- **Cocoa powder**

- **Honey or maple syrup**

- **Dark chocolate**, preferably 70 per cent cocoa or above.

Frozen foods

- **Frozen fruit**, like blueberries, cherries, pineapple, mango, banana and strawberries.

MEAL PLANNER WITH NON-UPF SNACKS, DRINKS, BREAKFASTS, LUNCHES, EVENING MEALS AND DESSERTS

A full meal weekly meal planner example! Hopefully it's not too overwhelming, given we have built it up gradually. I know some people don't have a sweet tooth, but I thought it would be good to include a dessert option for inspiration, as you never know when those cravings will hit. Feel free to ignore it, but it is here if you want it!

How Not to Eat Ultra-Processed

	Monday	Tuesday	Wednesday
Breakfast	Overnight oats (see recipe on page 136) with nut butter and banana	Butterbean shakshuka (see recipe on page 141)	Vegan oaty blueberry muffins (see recipe on page 134)
Morning snack	Apple and cheese	Oatcakes topped with nut butter and banana slices	Berries with plain yoghurt and a drizzle of honey if desired
Lunch	Pesto pasta Buddha bowl (see recipe on page 168)	Smashed avocado, feta and eggs on wholegrain bread (see recipe on page 174)	Tuna niçoise salad (see recipe on page 181)
Afternoon snack	Carrots and hummus – homemade (see recipe on page 85) or shop bought	Dark chocolate and coconut energy balls (see recipe on page 88)	Small bag of popcorn – or pop at home with kernels
Evening meal	Paneer curry (see recipe on page 219)	Herby cod with crispy potato traybake (see recipe on page 210)	Mixed bean chilli (see recipe on page 213)
Dessert/ evening snack	Fruit salad and plain yoghurt	Dark chocolate and almonds	Pear and almond traybake (see recipe on page 238)
Drinks	Water and warm golden milk with turmeric	Water and hot chocolate made from warm milk, cocoa powder and a dash of maple syrup	Water and strawberry- and cucumber- infused water

(Bonus) Week 5 – desserts

Thursday	Friday	Saturday	Sunday
Peanut butter and banana on wholegrain toast	Greek yoghurt pancakes (see recipe on page 132)	Sweet potato fritters (see recipe on page 139)	Spinach and mushroom omelette
Healthy trail mix – made from plain nuts, dried fruit and dark chocolate	Dried apricots and almonds	Medjool dates stuffed with nut butter and a little dark chocolate	Avocado on a wholegrain cracker with slices of boiled egg
Mediterranean mozzarella, pesto and tomato wrap (see recipe on page 179)	Carrot and lentil soup (see recipe on page 177)	Hummus with garlic and herb mushrooms on sourdough toast (see recipe on page 175)	Sunday dinner with all the trimmings
Roasted butter beans with olive oil and spices	No-bake fruit and oat bars (see recipe on page 90)	Pear and a handful of walnuts	Roasted kale crisps
Baked salmon with crunchy crispbread topping and sweet potato wedges (see recipe on page 208)	Vegetable noodle stir fry (see recipe on page 216)	Chicken fajitas with wholegrain wraps	Loaded jacket potatoes
Five-minute chocolate orange mug cake (see recipe on page 242)	Yoghurt with cocoa powder and honey	Cherry crumble (see recipe on page 236)	Healthier rocky road (see recipe on page 240)
Water and herbal tea of choice	Water and lemon, ginger and honey tea (see recipe on page 107)	Water and fresh carrot and orange juice (see recipe on page 105)	Water and date, banana and cocoa smoothie (see recipe on page 104)

YOUR FIVE-STEP HEALTHY CHECKLIST
FOR BONUS WEEK 5 (DESSERTS)

As in previous weeks, take a look at the goals below and choose which you would like to work on over the next few days and weeks.

Tick on the left if you want to work on a particular goal, and on the right when you have achieved it:

Tick to work on ✔	Goal	Tick when completed ✔
	Plan what nights you want to have a UPF dessert and the nights it's going to be homemade.	
	Have plain yoghurt with fresh or frozen fruit (plus honey if desired) for a quick and easy dessert option.	
	Pick a recipe from the ones in this chapter and have a go at making it this week!	
	Savour your dessert instead of watching something at the same time.	
	Add a portion of fruit or yoghurt to your next dessert.	

NON-UPF HEALTHY DESSERT RECIPES

Here are four of my favourite non-UPF healthy dessert recipes. Choose one or two and give them a go when a craving hits.

- Cherry crumble

- Pear and almond traybake

- Healthier rocky road

- Five-minute chocolate orange mug cake

CHERRY CRUMBLE

Vegan • **Serves:** 4 people • **Prep time:** 10 minutes
Cook time: 35–40 minutes

Homemade crumble is such a comforting pudding – and this recipe is one of my favourites because it makes the most of what you are likely to already have in your freezer and cupboards, only takes minutes to bring together *and* is vegan-friendly. Like most of my recipes, there is plenty of room to make this your own – you can switch up the cherries for frozen berries (blueberries or mixed berries work well) and the ground almonds for any blitzed nuts of your choice (hazelnuts are delicious – keep them a little chunkier if you like a crunchier crumble). I would definitely recommend adding the cornflour as frozen fruit can release a lot of liquid and it will help absorb excess moisture. It is perfect as it is, but I also like to serve it with yoghurt or, if I have the time, homemade custard.

Benefits: Cherries are rich in potassium, vitamin C, fibre and protective plant compounds to help promote good heart health. Nuts are an excellent source of plant-based protein, fibre and healthy fats, while olive oil is high in antioxidants and is a healthier alternative to butter.

For the fruit
500g frozen pitted sweet cherries
1–2 tbsp maple syrup, or to taste (optional)
1 tsp vanilla extract
1 tsp cornflour

For the crumble
100g plain or wholemeal flour
*75g ground almonds (add an extra 75g flour if making
   nut-free)*

½ tsp ground cinnamon, or to taste
45g rolled oats
60g maple syrup
1 tsp vanilla extract
4 tbsp olive oil

To serve
Plain yoghurt or homemade custard

1. Preheat the oven to 200°C/180°C fan.

2. Tip the frozen cherries into a medium-sized deep oven-proof dish (about 15cm×22cm×8cm). Drizzle over the maple syrup and vanilla extract. Mix well, taste and adjust the sweetness, if necessary. Sprinkle over the cornflour and mix to coat. Spread into an even layer. Set aside.

3. Add the flour, ground almonds, cinnamon and oats into a bowl and mix well. Add the maple syrup, vanilla extract and olive oil and mix well using a fork to combine – it will feel quite wet and sticky so use the fork to create more of a crumbly consistency.

4. Tip the crumble mix over the cherries and spread in an even layer to cover.

5. Bake in the oven for 35–40 minutes (the exact time will depend on the size, shape and depth of your dish) or until the fruit is bubbling and the topping is golden and crisp.

6. Remove from the oven and leave to stand for 5–10 minutes.

7. Serve with your choice of plain yoghurt or homemade custard.

Storage: Best served warm. Any baked leftovers can be left to cool completely before covering and chilling in the fridge for up to three days.

PEAR AND ALMOND TRAYBAKE

Vegetarian • **Makes:** 8–12 slices • **Prep time:** 10 minutes
Cook time: 25 minutes

Pears and almonds are a classic flavour combination found in many popular cakes and pastries. I have used this traditional pairing as the inspiration for my healthier traybake, which includes wholemeal flour for extra fibre, and olive oil instead of butter for a wonderfully moist texture (while keeping the saturated fats low). This is an incredibly simple recipe that requires no special equipment – and it can be adapted by using different fruits and nuts (ground hazelnuts and tinned apricots work well). I have included the option to add almond extract, if you like a stronger almond flavour, but you could also add vanilla extract for a subtle vanilla flavour, or keep it as it is – either way, it will still be utterly delicious. Thank you to my friend Louisa for inspiring this recipe addition!

Benefits: Wholemeal flour provides fibre and B vitamins for slow-release energy, while olive oil and almonds provide healthy monounsaturated fats and antioxidants.

For the traybake
130g wholemeal (or white if preferred) self-raising flour
70g ground almonds
100g caster sugar
125ml light olive oil
2 eggs, beaten
*A couple of drops of almond or vanilla extract, to taste
(optional)*
150g yoghurt of your choice
*1 tin (approximately 400g) of pear halves, in juice, drained
and sliced*

2 tbsp flaked almonds
1 tsp brown sugar

To serve (optional)
Icing sugar, to dust
Yoghurt

1. Preheat the oven to 200°C/180°C fan and grease and line a 21×27cm (8×10 inch) baking tin with non-stick baking paper.

2. Add the flour, ground almonds and caster sugar to a large bowl and stir to combine.

3. Next, add the olive oil and eggs and stir again. Once combined, add the almond or vanilla extract (optional) and yoghurt and mix until you have a smooth batter.

4. Spoon into the baking tin and smooth into an even layer with the back of a spatula.

5. Arrange the pear slices evenly across the top of the mixture. Sprinkle the flaked almonds and brown sugar over.

6. Place in the oven and bake for about 22–25 minutes, or until golden on top and a skewer inserted into the centre comes out clean. Leave to cool in the tin.

7. Remove from the tin, dust with a little icing sugar, if desired, slice into 8 to 12 squares and serve with yoghurt (optional).

Storage: Can be stored, well covered, in the fridge for up to a week. Alternatively, wrap individual slices and freeze for up to three months.

HEALTHIER ROCKY ROAD

Vegan • **Makes:** 12 squares • **Prep time:** 15 minutes
Chill time: 3 hours

Rocky road is a childhood favourite of mine, and is one of the first things I learnt to make. This recipe puts a healthier twist on the traditional version, by using rice cakes and a mixture of dried fruits and nuts for texture, and by omitting the marshmallows to reduce the UPFs. What's more, this version is also vegan-friendly, so it's perfect to make if you follow a vegan diet or want to share with friends and family who do. You can adjust the dried fruit (e.g. opt for sultanas, dried cherries or finely chopped prunes instead of raisins, cranberries or apricots) and nuts (e.g. roughly chopped hazelnuts, cashews or peanuts work well as alternatives to almonds) to really make this your own.

Benefits: Using a mixture of dried fruit and nuts helps add diversity to promote good gut health. Both fruit and nuts are good sources of fibre and contribute towards the recommended 30g a day that we should be having.

> 3 rice cakes (weighing about 22g total)
> 200g good-quality dark chocolate, at least 70% cocoa
>   solids, chopped into chunks
> 50g smooth almond butter (or other nut butter of your
>   choice)
> 15g maple syrup
> 40g dried cranberries or apricots
> 40g raisins
> 40g almonds, roughly chopped

1. Line an 18×8cm/7×7 inch square tin with non-stick baking paper.

2. Place the rice cakes into a freezer bag and carefully bash them up with a rolling pin. You want to have fairly small pieces, but there should still be some chunks (i.e. not bread-crumbs). Set aside.

3. In a bowl set over a pan of barely simmering water, melt the dark chocolate, stirring often, until glossy and smooth (alter-natively, place in a microwave-safe bowl and microwave in 30 second blasts, stirring in between each). Stir in the almond butter and maple syrup. Remove from the heat. Leave to cool for 5 minutes.

4. Stir in the dried cranberries, raisins, roughly chopped almonds and crushed rice cakes until these components are all totally coated in the chocolate. Pour into the prepared tin and smooth over the surface. Cover and chill for at least 3 hours, or until completely set.

5. Remove from the tin and, using a sharp knife, cut into 12 squares. Enjoy!

Top tip: Heating the blade of the knife before you cut the squares will help create cleaner slices

Storage: Keep in an airtight container in the fridge for up to a week. You may wish to remove the squares from the fridge 15–20 minutes before serving them (depending on the temperature of the room) to make them easier to eat.

FIVE-MINUTE CHOCOLATE ORANGE MUG CAKE

Vegetarian and vegan adaptable • **Makes:** 1 mug cake
Prep time: 5 minutes • **Cook time:** 1 minute

If you're anything like me then you'll enjoy having something sweet after your evening meal, and although those fancy desserts that you can buy in glass ramekins are delicious, they are quite expensive, and due to their nutritional profile should be enjoyed in moderation. This recipe though can be whipped up with ingredients that you may already have in your kitchen at a fraction of the cost (and added sugar!).

Top tip: if your cake sinks, try not over-mixing the batter, adjust the cooking settings according to the power of your microwave, and try using a different shaped/sized mug!

3 level tbsp (30g) self-raising flour
¼ tsp baking powder
2 tsp cocoa powder
1 tsp brown sugar
3–4 tbsp milk (of any kind)
Juice and zest of half an orange
1 tbsp chocolate chips
1 tsp marmalade (optional)
Sprinkle of icing sugar (optional)

1. Add the dry ingredients (except the chocolate chips) to a medium–large-sized mug and stir to combine.

2. Then, add the milk and orange juice and mix through until smooth.

3. Add the chocolate chips, mix again and then add a tsp of marmalade to the middle (optional), take a spoonful of the mixture and place on top so it's encased in the chocolate mix.

4. Pop in the microwave and heat for 60–90 seconds or until set on top (depending on the size of your mug – keep an eye out for when it may overflow!). Top with orange zest (and a dusting of optional icing sugar) and enjoy.

END OF BONUS WEEK 5 (DESSERTS) REFLECTION

Take a moment to consider how often you consume desserts, the types of desserts you choose, and whether you eat them mindfully.

Reflection questions

Have a think about your answers to the following questions:

- **Did you have a go at swapping a usual UPF dessert for a homemade option?** How did it taste in comparison?

- **How did you feel after consuming a UPF dessert versus a more nutritious homemade option?**

- **Were there any moments when you could have opted for a healthier alternative but chose a UPF dessert instead?** What would you do differently next time?

Remember, there are no right or wrong answers to these questions – just a chance to deep dive into the whats and whys of your eating habits, information that can help you to make better choices in the future.

So, what now? Firstly, congratulations and well done! You've completed a month of mindfully consuming fewer UPFs, which is a big step towards better health (both for your body and your mind). You should feel really proud of any changes that you have made so far, no matter how small, as it's the 'doing' and the consistency that matters most. Although we may be nearing the end of the book, keep in mind that this is just the start of your journey to a healthier dietary intake, and I want you to revisit this book many times as you start to look at the foods you eat with a more inquisitive eye. The following two chapters are important to read and will help you along your journey to consuming fewer UPFs overall.

PART THREE

LOOKING
AHEAD

CHAPTER 10

HOW NOT TO EAT ULTRA-PROCESSED ON A BUDGET

Well done on making it this far – it shows dedication to wanting to improve your dietary intake and health for the long term. In this chapter I want to share some essential strategies to support you in making healthier choices and reducing your UPFs one by one, no matter what your budget.

GENERAL MEAL PLANNING AND FOOD SHOPPING TIPS WHEN ON A BUDGET

Food shopping on a budget can make healthy eating seem out of reach. However, a little meal planning can help you reach your nutrition and health goals while also keeping your finances and food waste in check. Here are some tips for reducing your UPFs when on a budget:

1 **Write a meal plan and shopping list:** going shopping without a plan of meals you want to make for the week, and a subsequent shopping list, can set you up to be the victim of promotions for UPFs, and subjects you to food waste too. Make a meal plan consisting of nutritious meals for the week ahead and write a food shopping list. Plan to cook more than what you need, so you can have leftovers the following day or when you're short on time (cook once, eat twice!).

2 **Be savvy with ingredients:** when planning your weekly meals, try to overlap ingredients to avoid food waste – for example, can you use carrots in a Bolognese and in your morning snack? Spoiler alert: yes, you can! Or can you plan to have an omelette at the end of the week (don't forget to buy eggs!) to use up any leftover vegetables?

3 **Food shop at the right time:** align your supermarket shopping with times when stores offer discounts, typically towards the end of the day. Make sure to eat before you go shopping to avoid impulsive purchases driven by physical hunger.

4 **Think tinned and frozen for fruits and vegetables:** you will be pleased to know that it's not just fresh fruit and vegetables that count towards your five a day, as frozen, dried and tinned produce (which are often much more cost-effective and more nutritious too) also counts, so if you're on a budget or trying to save money, these are great choices. Choose fruit tinned in juice over syrup for less added sugar.

5 **Minimise food waste:** be creative with leftovers to avoid waste. Organise your fridge to prioritise items that need to be used first and consider freezing food for longer shelf life (peeled bananas freeze well and can be made into an ice cream!). If possible, start a small garden to grow your own herbs and vegetables, further reducing costs.

There's no need for superfoods. It can be easy to think that we need to eat so-called 'superfoods', such as expensive powders, to have a healthy diet, when in actual fact, there is no such thing as a superfood. The most important thing is that you're eating a wide variety of plants and whole foods within your diet, which can include nuts, seeds, wholegrains, tinned beans, lentils as well as fruits and vegetables, which are packed with nutrients such as fibre, protein and essential vitamins and minerals – yet they're only a fraction of the price of foods marketed as 'superfoods'.

TOP TIPS FOR SAVING MONEY WHEN BUYING WHOLE FOODS

- **Look for deals on fresh fruit and vegetables:** if you can't eat them all in a week, prep to freeze for later!

- **Choose (cheaper) 'wonky' veg:** because it's what's on the inside that counts!

- **Buy tins and spices from the 'world food' aisle:** you often get more for your money this way. Tinned tomatoes, coconut milk and beans are great staple items to have in.

- **Buy own-brand carbs (think rice, pasta and oats):** the ingredients and nutritional value is often the same (the only difference is the packaging!).

- **Go for tinned over fresh fish:** longer-life, tinned oily fish is still a great source of omega-3 fatty acids – essential for heart health. Aim for at least two portions of fish a week, one of which should be oily, such as salmon, mackerel or sardines.

- **Invest in dried lentils:** you can use them in stews, curries and soups to bulk up your recipes and make your meals go further.

- **Buy nuts from the baking aisle:** they're often cheaper and there's so much variety!

- **Don't buy bottled water or ice**: chill your water in a jug in the fridge on a daily basis if you don't like tap water. Infusing with herbs and fruits can also help.

- **Buy frozen berries and mixed frozen vegetables:** this is a cost-effective way to reach your five a day.

CHAPTER 11

CONCLUSION

Congratulations on coming to the end of this book, which has hopefully helped you to reflect on the areas of your diet where UPFs may be creeping in and, most importantly, how you can go about reducing your intake (particularly of the less-nutritious varieties). You may be feeling healthier thanks to the introduction of more whole foods and nutrients into your diet over the past month, but above all, I hope you feel clearer about what UPFs mean in today's modern society, and have learnt that healthy eating isn't about perfection, rather it's about finding the balance between eating to live and living to eat.

While the aim is always to reduce consumption of UPFs by making informed decisions regarding how we plan and use our time, and about which foods to buy when we are out, UPFs are not all created equal, particularly from a nutritional point of view. The majority of UPFs, including confectionery, pastries and fast food, are high in sugars, salts and unhealthy fats, and are low in nutrients, yet other UPFs such as omega-3 enriched fish fingers, tomato-based pasta sauces, wholegrain bread and baked beans are brimming with nutrition and can still feature as a part of a balanced lifestyle. The key is to look at the back of the pack and read the ingredients list, in addition to cooking or preparing more at home using single-ingredient whole foods, as we have discussed. It's about making healthier decisions more often, rather than never touching UPFs again.

The NOVA classification system, as discussed in Chapter 1 (Introduction to UPFs), describes how UPFs are defined, however we need to keep in mind that it was designed as a population-level tool – it wasn't designed to label individual foods as good or bad. A healthy diet is about the balance of nutrients that you are taking in over time, and although reducing your intake of UPFs can help with this, they do not need to be completely omitted, especially the more-nutritious varieties.

As also previously touched on, the Scientific Advisory Committee on Nutrition (SACN) highlights that food processing can have benefits like increasing shelf life, improving safety and even enhancing nutrient composition. But it also points out that a high intake of UPFs has been associated with poorer health outcomes, often due to the UPFs' nutritional profiles. It is important to note, however, that some studies were observational and didn't control for body mass index, smoking and socio-economic status, all of which are factors that can influence health in their own way. The take-away message is that our health depends on what we are eating and drinking the *majority* of the time, in addition to other lifestyle factors such as activity levels, sleep quality, social connections and stress management.

Did you know that some types of food processing actually *enhance* nutrient availability? An example of this is a phytochemical (healthy plant-chemical) called lycopene found in tomatoes, which is easier for our bodies to absorb when cooked (e.g. chopped tomatoes in a tin) versus when eaten raw. Another example is frozen vegetables and fruits, which often contain more vitamins, such as vitamin C, than their fresh equivalents, as they are frozen at the point of picking and therefore don't degrade over time.

Everyone has their own individual relationship with food, and labelling foods as good or bad isn't the way forward. Foods hold no moral value, and they do more than just nourish us physically. Food is more than just nutrients – it's about enjoyment, culture, and sometimes, convenience; I love a fish finger, oven chips or baked beans with (frozen) peas meal, and so do my children!

TEN OVERARCHING PRINCIPLES TO TAKE FORWARD TO HELP REDUCE YOUR INTAKE OF UPFs

The following is a summary of the points discussed throughout this book. I hope it serves as a useful reminder, but if questions arise on your journey to consuming fewer UPFs, remember that you can flick back to relevant weeks and sections as needed.

1 **Whole foods first:** prioritise foods that are in their most natural state. Think whole fruit and vegetables, wholegrains, fibrous or lean proteins such as beans, and healthy fats such as avocados and olive oil. This ensures you are getting maximum fibre and the nutrients needed for energy levels and healthy digestion too.

2 **Variety is key:** incorporate a wide variety of plants into your diet on a weekly basis – think fruits, vegetables, grains, nuts, seeds, pulses and legumes. Mixing up the colours and the types of fruits, vegetables and grains makes it more likely that you'll eat 30 different plant-based foods a week, which contributes to good health. (Remember, though, that variety means *all* foods, including those you enjoy, as your relationship with food is just as important as your nutritional intake.)

3 **Mindful eating:** pay attention to why and how you eat, not just what you eat. Savour each bite. Take your time, feel gratitude and notice how the flavours change as you

chew. This will also help you identify when you are physically full. This doesn't need to happen at every meal and snack (as this is unrealistic and could become obsessive), but start by limiting distractions at mealtimes, or by taking just a few mindful bites at the start of a meal if that is what works best for you.

4 **Hydration:** focus on having water as your primary drink, with herbal teas and sugar-free drinks as a second. This will support energy levels, hydrate the skin and ensure healthy digestion. Limit caffeine to the morning and early afternoon, so it doesn't impact your sleep, and reduce your consumption of sugary or ultra-processed drinks.

5 **Cooking matters:** prepare more meals at home, using whole foods, so you are in control of the ingredients used. This also means consuming fewer preservatives, emulsifiers and other additives. Cooking once so you can eat twice will save you time and energy also.

6 **Read labels:** understand and minimise your consumption of ultra-processed ingredients. Look out for key words outlined in the Appendix of this book – added sugars, high salt and fat levels – and try to choose food with more whole-food ingredients and shorter ingredients lists.

7 **Balance over perfection:** aim for sustainable changes, not restrictive diets, and follow the 80/20 rule. There's no need to cut out UPFs completely, although I would encourage you to have less of them, and to choose the more nutritious options where possible, balancing them out with whole foods.

8 **Listen to your body:** understand the different types of hunger (head, heart and stomach hunger as discussed in Chapter 3 [Let's get ready – the pre-plan plan]) and be aware of why you're eating – is it out of boredom, habit, pleasure or true stomach hunger? All types of hunger are valid, but get curious about how often you experience each type and how you can best meet your needs, including your emotional needs. Seek help from your GP or a mental health professional if you are struggling with this.

9 **Organise for success:** keep your kitchen stocked with healthy, whole-food options. Keeping your environment tidy will also boost energy and motivation levels to prepare more food.

10 **Reflect and adapt:** regularly assess your habits and adjust as needed. Reflect on what is working for you and what is not so you can brainstorm ideas, adjust and reap better results! If you are struggling with this, seek support from a Dietitian or a Registered Nutritionist.

So, what next? Keep a three- to seven-day food and drink diary during the week ahead and see how many of your drinks, meals and snacks are UPFs in comparison to when you first did this a month ago. You now have all the tools you need to reduce the number of UPFs in your diet in a sustainable and healthy way. I wish you all the best in your journey to reducing your consumption of UPFs, and here's to a healthier and happier future!

FOOD DIARY AND MEAL PLANNER TEMPLATE

Use two copies of the following blank template to not only record what you eat over the next week, but what you plan to eat too.

	Monday	Tuesday	Wednesday	
Breakfast				
Morning snack				
Lunch				
Afternoon snack				
Evening meal				
Dessert/ evening snack				
Drinks				

Conclusion

Thursday	Friday	Saturday	Sunday

WHICH FOODS ARE CLASSED AS UPFs?

Knowing which everyday foods you should be eating more of and less of can be confusing, so that's why I've done the legwork for you by coming up with a tiering system and guide based on food processing level *and* nutritional value too. This will enable you to understand which foods to prioritise on a day-to-day basis.

What follows is a description of the four groups included in the nutritionally tiered system, and how often to include them in order to achieve a healthy and balanced diet. The groups aren't meant to be a *strict* guide, or a reason to feel guilty if you do end up consuming more of the Group 4 foods and drinks than planned, they're simply a way of supporting you in making more informed food choices.

THE FOUR GROUPS IN
HOW NOT TO EAT ULTRA-PROCESSED

Group 1 – Unprocessed foods

These are whole foods in their natural state, such as fruits, vege-tables and potatoes, as well as grains such as oats and rice, and proteins including dried beans, fresh meat and fish. These foods have undergone minimal or no processing and are therefore high in nutrients (the only processing that they may have undergone is freezing, drying or packaging).

How often should I eat them? Unprocessed foods should make up the majority of your diet. Meals, including snacks, should be centred around this group, most of the time.

Group 2 – Minimally processed foods

This group includes foods like fruit juice and tinned beans that have been minimally processed to preserve and extend their shelf life, but which are still high in nutrients. They may have one or two added culinary ingredients or simply have added water. These foods are *not* classed as ultra-processed and do not, on the whole, need to be limited.

How often should I eat them? Consume these foods daily and most of them freely, but still be aware of how some processing methods impact the food, such as added sodium (salt) or sugar in some tinned goods (rinse before cooking), or reduced fibre in 100 per cent fruit juices (limit to 150ml a day), compared to whole fruits.

Group 3 – More-processed yet nutritious UPFs

These foods and drinks are technically classed as ultra-processed, but still offer nutritional value and a high level of micronutrients, such as vitamins and minerals, in addition to protein and fibre, for example, frozen fish fingers, most supermarket bread, tinned baked beans and carton oat milk. Some of these items may be extremely useful and relied upon in diets that are limited due to food allergies or intolerances. These foods may contain added ingredients for preservation, taste and texture, in addition to vitamins too – skip to the end of the Appendix for more information on this.

How often should I eat them? Incorporate these foods into your diet in moderation alongside whole foods, and use them where allergies or intolerances make them a necessity. They can be convenient when you're busy and have little time to prepare food, or when fresh food is scarce in your fridge, but do try to balance them with foods from Groups 1 and 2 for optimal overall health.

Group 4 – More-processed and less-nutritious UPFs

These are the classic UPFs that we should ideally be cutting down on and consuming on an infrequent basis. Foods in this category, such as chocolate biscuits, oven chips and crisps, are highly processed and are often high in added sugars, unhealthy fats and salt, while being low in essential nutrients. They may also be known as HFSS (high in fat, sugar and salt).

How often should I eat them? View these foods as 'fun foods' or 'soul foods' and eat them purely for enjoyment. They should not make up the bulk of your diet or fuel your day. Savour these foods when you do have them. These foods (and drinks) are the 20 per cent of the 80/20 rule, as discussed in the introduction.

FIVE WAYS TO IDENTIFY UPFs

Here are five things to look for if you're actively trying to reduce your consumption of UPFs:

1 **A long ingredients list:** a long list of ingredients *may* indicate that the food or drink in question is a UPF. This is especially true if some of the ingredients are not found in your kitchen, but only in food produced by food manufacturers.

Look for words such as 'concentrates', 'modified starch', 'emulsifiers', 'thickeners', 'E-numbers', 'flavour enhancers' and 'colours' on the ingredients list, and think twice before you buy – is there an alternative that you can buy instead, or could you make something at home? **Please note:** some foods such as breakfast cereals may have a long ingredients list due to fortification (i.e. added vitamins and minerals), which is not unhealthy. Check out the end of the Appendix for more information.

2 **An unrecognisable ingredient:** if the ingredient is unrecognisable, it could be an additive. Food additives are safe to consume, and while you don't need to eliminate them entirely, if you are consuming a large number of foods containing them, it might be a sign you've got a lot of UPFs in your diet. Consuming more foods from Groups 1 and 2 will naturally decrease your additive intake.

3 **Look at the traffic light guide:** look for ambers and reds. UPFs are often red for fat, salt and sugar, however not all food manufacturers choose to use a colourful food labelling system. The only way you will know if a food is a UPF or not is to look at the ingredients list, which is listed from biggest to smallest ingredient. **Please note:** some whole foods may present as red on the traffic light label, for example nuts and oily fish for healthy fats, or dried fruit for sugar – this does not make them unhealthy, far from it. And some UPFs may be green, such as sweets for fat or diet cola for sugar – this does not mean that they are nutritious or are a whole food. Context matters.

4 **If it has a long shelf life:** a long shelf life likely indicates that a food contains preservatives, but it doesn't always mean that the food is a UPF. For example, bacon has salt and nitrates but is not technically a UPF (however it should still be consumed in moderation as discussed previously), whereas most supermarket salami *is* classed as a UPF due to the added ingredients and further processing. Long-life milk has been pasteurised at high temperatures, making it processed, but is not a UPF as no preservatives have been added. Common preservatives include sodium benzoate, nitrates and sulfites, Butylated hydroxyanisole (BHA) and butylated hydroxytoluene (BHT). **Please note:** ascorbic acid (vitamin C) is a natural preservative, but when added does not automatically turn the food into a UPF.

5 **The food has multi-coloured packaging:** if there is a big marketing campaign for a product then it could be a UPF. Have you ever seen a high-end marketing campaign for plums? Likely not. Some foods though are of course an exception, for example, branded wheat biscuits (which are not a UPF), not mentioning any names!

Certain emulsifiers found in UPFs have been linked with irritable bowel disease (IBD), and three in particular have been highlighted. Initial research has been done in rodents, however, and it's not known yet how they will impact people – research is currently underway. These emulsifiers aren't commonly found in the UK, however if you do find them in a product that you consume on a regular basis, it may be advisable to reduce the frequency in which you have it.

- Polysorbate 80 (P80) or E433

- Carrageenan or E407

- Carboxymethyl cellulose (CMC) or E466

COMMONLY EATEN FOODS IN ALPHABETICAL ORDER

Remember, what matters most is what you are eating and drinking most of the time – focus on Groups 1 and 2 where possible, and choose foods in Group 3 over Group 4.

IMPORTANT POINTS

The following table is not a reflection of the NOVA classification of foods (as discussed in Chapters 1 and 11), instead, it is a way of classifying foods according to their level of processing *plus* nutritional value (or in some cases, added sugar content) when it comes to UPFs. NOVA's definition of UPFs has been used though, to help categorise foods that fall into Groups 3 and 4.

This table is a guide, and isn't intended to be a black and white list of rules to follow, as individual context matters, for example, a flavoured milkshake could be a very nutritious choice for someone with a poor appetite, a low calcium intake or for someone who is trying to gain weight.

Individuality matters and the advice in this table should not be used in the place of tailored advice from a healthcare professional, as discussed at the start of this book.

Food type	Group 1 (unprocessed or minimally processed) – eat mostly
Fruit and vegetables Fruits and vegetables provide us with fibre, antioxidants, vitamins and minerals that we need for good health, including supporting the immune system. We should consume at least five portions a day (fresh, frozen or tinned), a portion being 80g (a handful or three tablespoons) or 30g of dried fruit.	All 100 per cent whole fruits and vegetables (fresh, frozen or dried) For example: • Apples, apricots, asparagus, avocados • Bananas, beetroots, bell peppers, berries (all), broccoli, butternut squash • Cabbage, carrots, cauliflower, cherries, courgettes, cucumbers • Garlic, grapefruit, grapes, green beans • Herbs and spices (dried or fresh) • Kale, kiwi • Lemons, lettuce, limes • Mangoes, mixed salad leaves, mushrooms • Olives, onions, oranges • Papaya, peaches, pears, peas, pineapple, plums, pumpkin • Radishes, raisins • Spinach, sweetcorn, sweet potatoes • Tomatoes • Watermelon

Commonly eaten foods in alphabetical order

Group 2 (processed in some way) – eat most of these freely	Group 3 (more-nutritious UPFs) – eat some	Group 4 (less-nutritious UPFs) – eat least
• Guacamole (shop bought – look for fewer ingredients, some may contain ascorbic acid as an antioxidant, which is vitamin C) • Soups – most fresh soups containing whole-food ingredients • Sun-dried tomatoes (jarred) • Tinned fruit in natural juice (limit juice to 150ml) • Tinned tomatoes (citric acid is a compound from fruit) • Tinned vegetables (e.g. sweetcorn) • Tomato-based sauce (some – based on whole foods) • Tomato ketchup (with whole-food ingredients) – use in moderation due to concentrated sugars • Tomato purée	• Dried fruit with added preservatives and oils or added sugar • Salsa (most jarred as well as fresh shop-bought varieties) • Soups – tinned soups based on vegetables (plants) but containing ingredients such as modified corn starch and milk proteins • Tomato-based sauce (some – with added ingredients not usually found in a home kitchen) • Tomato ketchup (with ingredients such as modified maize starch and flavourings) • Vegetable burgers – fresh or frozen (ingredients lists will vary and some may fall into Group 4)	• Tinned soups higher in salt (red on the label for salt) or saturated fat (red on the label for saturated fat) that contain ingredients not usually found in a home kitchen

Food type	Group 1 (unprocessed or minimally processed) – eat mostly	Group 2 (processed in some way) – eat most of these freely
Starchy carbs This is the body's preferred energy source. Choose wholegrain options for more fibre. *Some starchy carbs may feature in the protein section due to the nature of their macronutrient content.*	Most wholegrains including: • Barley • Buckwheat • Oats • Popcorn kernels • Quinoa (dried) • Rice (basmati, brown, wild) • Granola (homemade) • Plantain • Potatoes • Yam	• Breads – those not containing additional additives such as emulsifiers (e.g. shop-bought traditionally made sourdough bread, rye bread and some wholemeal supermarket loaves, bagels and wraps), ideally choose wholemeal • Breakfast cereals (shop bought, containing only whole foods, ideally wholegrain and added vitamins) • Buckwheat noodles • Bulgur wheat • Couscous • Granola (shop bought containing only whole foods) • Pasta – brown will provide more fibre • Popcorn (pre-popped but minimal ingredients) • Quinoa (pre-cooked in a pouch) • Ravioli (containing only whole foods) • Rice – white and pre-cooked • Rice cakes – with minimal ingredients • Snack bars (containing only whole foods) • Wholegrain crackers – with minimal ingredients • (100 per cent) Wholewheat biscuits

Commonly eaten foods in alphabetical order

Group 3 (more-nutritious UPFs) – eat some	Group 4 (less-nutritious UPFs) – eat least
• Breads – those containing additional additives such as emulsifiers (including sliced bread, bagels and wraps), ideally choose wholemeal • Breakfast cereals (not coated in sugar, chocolate or honey, containing ingredients not usually found in a home kitchen) • Microwave ready meals (fresh and frozen) – those rich in vegetables, wholegrains and lean protein • Noodles (most that cook within minutes) • Pizza (shop bought – mostly greens on the traffic label, e.g. thin crust, loaded with vegetables) • Popcorn (shop bought, with long ingredients list featuring substances not usually found in a home kitchen) • Ravioli (containing ingredients such as modified corn flour) • Sandwiches (ready-made and shop bought on brown bread with salad and lean protein) • Snack bars (main ingredients are oats, nuts and dried fruit, plus ingredients not usually found in a home kitchen)	• Breakfast cereals (coated in sugar, chocolate or honey and with ingredients not usually found in a home kitchen) • Chips (most frozen, some may fall into Group 2 if they have minimal ingredients) • Microwave ready meals (fresh and frozen) – those lacking in vegetables, wholegrains and lean protein • Noodles – pre-flavoured (instant or pot) • Pizza (shop bought – mostly reds on the traffic label, e.g. thick crust with extra cheese and red meat) • Popcorn (shop bought, coated in butter or sugar, plus other ingredients not usually found in a home kitchen) • Potato waffles (usually frozen) • Potato wedges (most frozen varieties) • Sandwiches (ready-made and shop bought on white bread with red meat) – mostly red on traffic light, e.g. for saturated fat and salt • Snack bars – first ingredients being sugar or syrup or chocolate plus others not found in a home kitchen

Food type	Group 1 (unprocessed or minimally processed) – eat mostly	Group 2 (processed in some way) – eat most of these freely
Protein Protein is essential for building muscle and repairing tissue. Protein requirements vary depending on the individual and their activity levels, but usually ranges from 0.8g to 2g of protein per Kg of body weight a day. Prioritise plant protein when able. *Some proteins may feature in the carbs section due to the nature of their macronutrient content.*	• Beans (dried) • Beef* – choose leaner varieties, i.e. less than 5 per cent fat • Chicken – leaner cuts include breast • Chickpeas (dried) • Eggs • Fish and shellfish (fresh or frozen, e.g. cod, haddock, prawns, salmon or sardines) • Hummus (homemade) • Lamb* (fresh, choose leaner cuts) • Lentils (dried) • Milk (dairy) • Pork* (fresh, choose leaner cuts) • Turkey (fresh) • Tzatziki (homemade) • Yoghurt – plain e.g. Greek	• Beans (tinned), e.g. black beans, butter beans, cannellini beans, kidney beans and mixed beans (plus some tinned baked beans containing only whole foods) • Burgers (made from lean meat at butchers) • Cheese (plain) • Crème fraîche (most) • Chickpeas (tinned) • Falafel (shop bought made with whole foods) • Fish (tinned) e.g., mackerel, sardines and tuna – choose those in spring water or tomatoes over brine or oil • Hummus (most shop bought, minimal ingredients) • Lentils (pre-cooked and tinned or in a pouch) • Nutritional yeast • Tofu (plain) • Tzatziki, shop bought

* *Beef, lamb and pork, including bacon and sausages, are classified as red meat. Bacon is not technically classified as a UPF, but due to the processing and sodium (salt) levels, it is advised that it be limited as it is a processed red meat. Current guidelines advise us to have no*

Group 3 (more-nutritious UPFs) – eat some	Group 4 (less-nutritious UPFs) – eat least
• Baked beans (most tinned varieties) • Breaded fish or chicken (fresh or frozen) – choose those with a higher percentage of fish or chicken • Cream cheese (most) • Crème fraîche (some low-fat varieties) • Falafel (shop bought containing ingredients not usually found in home kitchen) • Hummus (some, which contain preservatives such as potassium sorbate) • Most foods containing Mycoprotein as the main ingredient • Tofu (shop bought and pre-marinated) • Yoghurts – low calorie (lower added sugar), fruit flavoured	• Bacon* • Battered fish or chicken (often much higher in fat and salt than breaded varieties) • Burgers (shop bought or fast food) • Cheese slices (highly processed, rubbery cheese slices, individually wrapped) • Chorizo (most) • Ham (most shop bought) • Hot dogs (jarred) • Meat pies • Salami • Sausages (most shop bought, some without additives may fall into Group 2) • Yoghurt – high in added sugar (fruit or chocolate corner pots)

more than 490g of cooked red and processed meat in total a week (or no more than 70g a day). Choose leaner cuts where possible, or drain any fat at home when cooking.

Food type	Group 1 (unprocessed or minimally processed) – eat mostly
Fats Essential for brain and heart health, as well as for the absorption of fat-soluble vitamins (A, D, E and K). Choose mainly healthy unsaturated fats such as olive oil, avocado, nuts and seeds. *Use fats in moderation due to their energy density (e.g. half to one tablespoon per person per meal).*	• Nuts (all plain), including: almonds, cashews, macadamia, peanuts and walnuts • Nut and seed butters (all 100 per cent nut and seed butters), e.g. peanut, almond or tahini (sesame seeds) • Olive oil (extra virgin) • Pesto (homemade) • Rapeseed oil (cold pressed) • Seeds (all plain), e.g. chia, pumpkin, sunflower
Sugars Keep free-sugar intake to under 30g a day (this includes added sugar as well as sugar in fruit juice and honey).	

Commonly eaten foods in alphabetical order

Group 2 (processed in some way) – eat most of these freely	Group 3 (more-nutritious UPFs) – eat some	Group 4 (less-nutritious UPFs) – eat least
• Butter (limit usage due to high saturated fat content) • Coconut oil (limit usage due to high saturated fat content) • Cream (limit usage due to saturated fat) • Olive oil (refined – good for cooking at higher temperatures) • Rapeseed oil (refined – good for cooking at higher temperatures) • Sunflower oil (not as high in monounsaturated fatty acids as olive oil or rapeseed oil)	• Coleslaw (homemade with shop-bought mayonnaise) • Dark chocolate (ideally choose 70 per cent or higher cocoa levels – note that those containing only whole foods will fall into Group 2) • Pesto – shop bought, containing additives • Spreads based on olive oil or vegetable oil (limit usage due to high calorie content)	• Biscuits • Buns (cupcakes) • Cakes • Cheese- or cream-based sauces • Chocolate (dairy, white or vegan) and chocolate bars • Creamy coleslaw (shop bought containing ingredients such as stabilisers e.g. guar gum and thickener e.g. pectin) • Crisps (most) • Croissants (shop bought) • Ice cream • Salad dressings and mayonnaise (most – use sparingly)
• Agave syrup • Cane sugar (table sugar) • Date syrup • Honey • Maple syrup • Sugar All of the above count as free-sugar, so consume in moderation.	• Jam – less sugar • Jelly – less sugar • Sweeteners (natural, e.g. stevia or xylitol) – not more nutritious but they are less energy dense and kinder to teeth than sugar.	• Ice lollies (most) • Jam – full sugar • Jelly – full sugar • Sweeteners (artificial) • Sweets (candy)

Food type	Group 1 (unprocessed or minimally processed) – eat mostly	Group 2 (processed in some way) – eat most of these freely
Drinks Aim to drink at least six to eight glasses of sugar-free fluids a day and aim to have no more than 300mg to 400mg of caffeine a day (or 200mg if you are pregnant or breastfeeding).	• Carbonated mineral water • Coffee granules • Milk (dairy) • Smoothies (homemade) • Spring water • Tap water • Teas – black, fruit and herbal	• Cocoa powder • (100 per cent) Fresh fruit or vegetable juice – limit to 150ml a day • Kefir (fermented milk drink) • Smoothies (shop bought) – limit to 150ml a day

Baby formula has not been included in this table as it is a safe nutrition source for babies.

Group 3 (more-nutritious UPFs) – eat some	Group 4 (less-nutritious UPFs) – eat least
• Flavoured water (sugar free) – not more nutritious but they are less energy dense and kinder to teeth than sugar • Fortified plant-based milks (e.g. almond, oat or soya milk, choose no added sugar if possible) • Meal replacement drinks (choose lower-sugar options where possible) • Protein shakes (with minimal ingredients and no added sugar) • Sodas (diet) – not more nutritious but they are less energy dense and kinder to teeth than sugar • Sports drinks (isotonic)	• Alcoholic beverages (most) • Energy drinks – often high in sugar • Flavoured coffee – with creamers and syrups • Flavoured sugary milkshakes • Flavoured waters with added sugar • Fruit juice drinks (with added sugar and sweetener) • Hot chocolate powder (most) • Iced tea (shop bought) • Sodas (regular)

GET TO KNOW YOUR VITAMINS

Reading the back of packs can feel like swimming against the current, and it can be tiring and overwhelming. With long unfamiliar words, it can seem like every ingredient is a foreign chemical, which isn't necessarily a bad thing! Some of these unique terms are actually vitamins and they are perfectly good for you – for example, ascorbic acid is vitamin C, which helps support a healthy immune system.

Here is some more information to help you understand these terms so you can be empowered to make good decisions when shopping.

TERMS ASSOCIATED WITH VITAMINS, AND THEREFORE NOT TO BE AVOIDED

Term	What is it?	Benefits*
Retinyl palmitate	Vitamin A	Needed for vision, skin health and the immune system
Thiamine mononitrate	Vitamin B1	Needed for the nervous system and to help make energy from the food we eat
Riboflavin	Vitamin B2	Plays a role in energy production, skin, eye and nervous system health
Niacinamide	Vitamin B3	Helps to release energy from food and supports the digestive system, nervous system and skin
Calcium pantothenate	Vitamin B5	Needed for releasing energy from food as well as hormone and cholesterol production
Pyridoxine hydrochloride	Vitamin B6	Involved in many enzyme reactions, nervous and immune system functions and in creating haemoglobin
Folic acid	Vitamin B9	Key for brain and spine development and making DNA
Cyanocobalamin	Vitamin B12	Needed for the nervous system and to help make red blood cells and DNA

* These nutrients have numerous functions and benefits. I have narrowed this down and highlighted the key benefits in this table.

Get to know your vitamins

Term	What is it?	Benefits*
Ascorbic acid	Vitamin C	Helps with iron absorption and plays a role in immunity and keeping tissues healthy (like skin and blood vessels)
Calciferol and Cholecalciferol	Vitamin D	Good for bone health, absorbing calcium and the immune system
Tocopherols (alpha-tocopherol)	Vitamin E	A fat-soluble vitamin, good for skin health and an antioxidant that protects the body from oxidative stress

REFERENCES

CHAPTERS 1–4 (ALSO REFERRED TO IN CHAPTER 10, CONCLUSION AND APPENDIX)

Acceptable daily intake (no date) European Food Safety Authority. [Accessed: March 2024 via https://www.efsa.europa.eu/en/glossary/acceptable-daily-intake]

Bancil, A., et al. (2021) Food Additive Emulsifiers and Their Impact on Gut Microbiome, Permeability, and Inflammation: Mechanistic Insights in Inflammatory Bowel Disease. [Accessed: March 2024 via https://pubmed.ncbi.nlm.nih.gov/33336247/]

Barbaresko, J. et al. (2024) Ultra-processed food consumption and human health: an umbrella review of systematic reviews with meta-analyses. [Accessed: March 2024 via https://pubmed.ncbi.nlm.nih.gov/38363072/]

BDA on Restricting Energy Drinks (2024) [Accessed: March 23, 2024 via https://www.bda.uk.com/resource/bda-supports-call-for-restricting-the-sale-and-marketing-of-energy-drinks-to-children-and-young-people.html]

BDA Policy Statement on Artificial Sweeteners (2016) [Accessed: March 2024 via https://www.bda.uk.com/static/11ea5867-96eb-43df-b61f2cbe9673530d/policystatementsweetners.pdf]

Bite Back 2030. (n.d.) Don't Hide What's Inside – Bite Back Campaign Report on Health Halo Claims [Accessed: March 23, 2024 via https://biteback.contentfiles.net/media/documents/Dont_Hide_Whats_Inside.pdf]

Blundell, J., and Finlayson, G. (2004) Is susceptibility to weight gain characterised by homeostatic or hedonic risk factors for overconsumption? [Accessed: March 2024 via https://pubmed.ncbi.nlm.nih.gov/15234585/]

Borsani, B., et al. (2021) The Role of Carrageenan in Inflammatory Bowel Diseases and Allergic Reactions: Where Do We Stand? [Accessed: March 2024 via https://www.ncbi.nlm.nih.gov/pmc/articles/PMC8539934/]

Braesco, V., et al. (2022). Ultra-processed foods: how functional is the NOVA system? [Accessed: March 2024 via https://doi.org/10.1038/s41430-022-01099-1]

BDA Iron Food Fact Sheet (2021) [Accessed: March 2024 via https://www.bda.uk.com/resource/iron-rich-foods-iron-deficiency.html]

Chassaing, B., et al. (2017) Dietary emulsifiers directly alter human microbiota composition and gene expression ex vivo potentiating intestinal inflammation. Gut. [Accessed: March 2024 via https://pubmed.ncbi.nlm.nih.gov/28325746/]

Chassaing, B., et al. (2022) Randomised Controlled-Feeding Study of Dietary Emulsifier Carboxymethylcellulose Reveals Detrimental Impacts on the Human Gut Microbiome and Metabolome. Gastroenterology. [Accessed: March 2024 via https://pubmed.ncbi.nlm.nih.gov/34774538/]

Cox, S., et al. (2021) Food additive emulsifiers: a review of their role in foods, legislation and classifications, presence in food supply, dietary exposure, and safety assessment [Accessed: March 2024 via https://pubmed.ncbi.nlm.nih.gov/32626902/]

Craig, W., et al. (2021). The Safe and Effective Use of Plant-Based

References

Diets with Guidelines for Health Professionals [Accessed: March 2024 via https://pubmed.ncbi.nlm.nih.gov/34836399/]

Dicken, S., et al. (2024) Nutrients or processing? An analysis of food and drink items from the UK National Diet and Nutrition Survey based on nutrient content, the NOVA classification and front of package traffic light labelling. British Journal of Nutrition. [Accessed: March 2024 via https://pubmed.ncbi.nlm.nih.gov/38220223/]

Dinu, M., et al. (2017) Vegetarian, vegan diets and multiple health outcomes: A systematic review with meta-analysis of observational studies [Accessed: March 2024 via https://pubmed.ncbi.nlm.nih.gov/26853923/]

Dixon, K., et al. (2023) Modern Diets and the Health of Our Planet: An Investigation into the Environmental Impacts of Food Choices [Accessed: March 2024 via https://pubmed.ncbi.nlm.nih.gov/36771398/]

Drewnowski, A. (2010) The Nutrient Rich Foods Index helps to identify healthy, affordable foods. [Accessed: March 2024 via https://pubmed.ncbi.nlm.nih.gov/20181811/]

Elizabeth, L., et al. (2020) Ultra-Processed Foods and Health Outcomes: A Narrative Review. [Accessed: March 2024 via https://pubmed.ncbi.nlm.nih.gov/32630022/]

FAO (2019) Report on Ultra-processed foods, diet quality, and health using the NOVA classification system: [Accessed: March 2024 via https://www.fao.org/3/ca5644en/ca5644en.pdf]

FDF – HFSS Toolkit: [Accessed: March 2024 via https://www.fdf.org.uk/fdf/resources/toolkits/diet-and-health/hfss-toolkit/#:~:text=The%20nutrient%20profile%20model%20is,to%20calculate%20your%20HFSS%20score]

Fiolet, T., et al. (2018) Consumption of ultra-processed foods and cancer risk: results from NutriNet-Santé prospective cohort. [Accessed: March 2024 via https://pubmed.ncbi.nlm.nih.gov/29444771/]

Gerasimidis, K., et al. (2020) The impact of food additives, artificial sweeteners and domestic hygiene products on the human gut microbiome and its fibre fermentation capacity. Eur J Nutr [Accessed: March 2024 via https://doi.org/10.1007/s00394-019-02161-8]

Hall, K., et al. (2019) Ultra-processed diets cause excess calorie intake and weight gain: An inpatient randomised controlled trial of ad libitum food intake. [Accessed: March 2024 via https://www.ncbi.nlm.nih.gov/pmc/articles/PMC7946062/]

Howard, S., et al. (2012) Nutritional content of supermarket ready meals and recipes by television chefs in the United Kingdom: Cross Sectional Study, BMJ. [Accessed: March 2024 via https://doi.org/10.1136/bmj.e7607]

Jardim, M., et al. (2021) Ultra-processed foods increase noncommunicable chronic disease risk . [Accessed: March 2024 via https://pubmed.ncbi.nlm.nih.gov/34798466/]

Kau, A., et al. (2011) Human nutrition, the gut microbiome, and immune system: envisioning the future [Accessed: March 2024 via https://www.ncbi.nlm.nih.gov/pmc/articles/PMC3298082/]

Kumar, A., et al. (2023) Gut Microbiota in Anxiety and Depression: Unveiling the Relationships and Management Options [Accessed: March 2024 via https://www.ncbi.nlm.nih.gov/pmc/articles/PMC10146621/]

Lane, M., et al. (2024) Ultra-processed food exposure and adverse health outcomes: umbrella review of epidemiological meta-analyses. The BMJ [Accessed: March 2024 via https://www.bmj.com/content/384/bmj-2023-077310]

Madruga, M. et al. (2023). Trends in food consumption according to the degree of food processing among the UK population over 11 years. British Journal of Nutrition. [Accessed: March 2024 via https://pubmed.ncbi.nlm.nih.gov/36259459/]

McDonald, D., et al. (2018) American Gut: an Open Platform for

References

Citizen Science Microbiome Research [Accessed: March 2024 via https://journals.asm.org/doi/10.1128/msystems.00031-18]

Monteiro, C., et al. (2018) The UN Decade of Nutrition, the NOVA food classification and the trouble with ultra-processing. Public Health Nutr. [Accessed: March 2024 via https://www.ncbi.nlm.nih.gov/pmc/articles/PMC10261019/]

Monteiro, C., et al. (2019) Ultra-processed foods: what they are and how to identify them. [Accessed: March 2024 via https://pubmed.ncbi.nlm.nih.gov/30744710]

Narula, N., et al. (2021) Association of ultra-processed food intake with risk of inflammatory bowel disease: prospective cohort study. [Accessed: March 2024 via https://doi.org/10.1136/bmj.n1554]

NHS Fat Guidelines [Accessed: March 2024 via https://www.nhs.uk/live-well/eat-well/food-types/different-fats-nutrition/]

NHS Sugar Guidelines [Accessed: March 2024 via https://www.nhs.uk/live-well/eat-well/food-types/how-does-sugar-in-our-diet-affect-our-health/]

NIH (2023) Calcium Fact Sheet for Health Professionals [Accessed: March 2024 https://ods.od.nih.gov/factsheets/Calcium-Health Professional/]

NIH (2023) Vitamin B12 Fact Sheet for Health Professionals [Accessed: March 2024 https://ods.od.nih.gov/factsheets/VitaminB12-HealthProfessional/]

Olson, R., et al. (2021) Food fortification: The advantages, disadvantages and lessons from sight and Life Programs. [Accessed: March 2024 via https://doi.org/10.3390/nu13041118]

Price, E., et al. (2024) Excluding whole grain-containing foods from the Nova ultraprocessed food category: a cross-sectional analysis of the impact on associations with cardiometabolic risk measures. [Accessed: March 2024 via https://pubmed.ncbi.nlm.nih.gov/38417577/]

Rauber, F., et al. (2018) Ultra-processed food consumption and chronic non-communicable diseases-related dietary nutrient profile in the UK (2008–2014) [Accessed: March 2024 via https://doi.org/10.3390/nu10050587]

Rauber, F., et al. (2020) Ultra-processed food consumption and indicators of obesity in the United Kingdom population (2008-2016) [Accessed: March 2024 via https://journals.plos.org/plosone/article?id=10.1371/journal.pone.0232676]

Rickman, J., Barrett, D., and Bruhn, C. (2007) Nutritional comparison of fresh, frozen and canned fruits and vegetables. part 1. vitamins C and B and phenolic compounds, Journal of the Science of Food and Agriculture. [Accessed: March 2024 via https://doi.org/10.1002/jsfa.2825]

Rico-Campà, A., et al. (2019) Association between consumption of ultra-processed foods and all cause mortality: Sun Prospective Cohort Study. [Accessed: March 2024 via https://doi.org/10.1136/bmj.l1949]

Rinninella, E., et al. (2020) Additives, Gut Microbiota, and Irritable Bowel Syndrome: A Hidden Track. [Accessed: March 2024 via https://www.ncbi.nlm.nih.gov/pmc/articles/PMC7730902/]

Roberts, C., et al. (2013) Hypothesis: Increased consumption of emulsifiers as an explanation for the rising incidence of Crohn's disease. [Accessed: March 2024 via https://pubmed.ncbi.nlm.nih.gov/23360575/]

SACN (2023) Statement on processed foods and health [Accessed: March 2024 via https://www.gov.uk/government/publications/sacn-statement-on-processed-foods-and-health/sacn-statement-on-processed-foods-and-health-summary-report]

Sanchez-Siles, L., et al. (2022) Naturalness and healthiness in "ultra-processed foods": A multidisciplinary perspective and case study. [Accessed: March 2024 via https://www.science direct.com/science/article/abs/pii/S0924224422004459]

Whelan, K., et al. (2024) Ultra-processed foods and food additives in gut health and disease [Accessed: March 2024 via https://pubmed.ncbi.nlm.nih.gov/38388570/]

Zhang, Y. and Giovannucci, E. (2023) Ultra-processed foods and health: a comprehensive review. [Accessed: March 2024 via https://pubmed.ncbi.nlm.nih.gov/35658669/]

No authors listed (2019) In Health effects of dietary risks in 195 countries, 1990–2017: a systematic analysis for the Global Burden of Disease Study 2017 [Accessed: March 2024 via https://pubmed.ncbi.nlm.nih.gov/30954305/]

CHAPTER 5

BDA Coffee and Health by Dr Duane Mellor RD (2019) [Accessed: March 2024 via https://www.bda.uk.com/resource/coffee-and-health-it-s-not-just-about-the-caffeine.html]

Crimarco, A., Landry, M., and Gardner, C. (2022) Ultra-processed Foods, Weight Gain, and Co-morbidity Risk. [Accessed: March 2024 via https://pubmed.ncbi.nlm.nih.gov/34677812/]

Food Standards Agency (FSA) – Food additives (2024) [Accessed: March 2024 via https://www.food.gov.uk/safety-hygiene/food-additives]

Heriseanu, A., et al. (2017) Grazing in adults with obesity and eating disorders: A systematic review of associated clinical features and meta-analysis of prevalence [Accessed: March 2024 via https://www.sciencedirect.com/science/article/abs/pii/S027273581630527X?via%3Dihub]

Marx, B., et al. (2016) Mechanisms of caffeine-induced diuresis. Médecine sciences, [Accessed: March 2024 via https://www.ncbi.nlm.nih.gov/pubmed/27225921]

Maughan, R., and Griffin, J. (2003) Caffeine ingestion and fluid balance: a review [Accessed: March 2024 via https://pubmed.ncbi.nlm.nih.gov/19774754/]

NHS Water, drinks and hydration [Accessed: March 2024 via https://www.nhs.uk/live-well/eat-well/food-guidelines-and-food-labels/water-drinks-nutrition/]

NIH (2023) Iodine Fact Sheet for Health Professionals [Accessed: March 2024 https://ods.od.nih.gov/factsheets/Iodine-Health Professional/]

Smith, H., et al. (2020) Glucose control upon waking is unaffected by hourly sleep fragmentation during the night, but is impaired by morning caffeinated coffee. [Accessed: March 2024 via https://pubmed.ncbi.nlm.nih.gov/32475359/]

CHAPTER 6

Appleton, J. (2018) The Gut-Brain Axis: Influence of Microbiota on Mood and Mental Health. [Accessed: March 2024 via https://www.ncbi.nlm.nih.gov/pmc/articles/PMC6469458/]

Gill, S. et al. (2020) Dietary fibre in gastrointestinal health and disease [Accessed: March 2024 via https://www.nature.com/articles/s41575-020-00375-4]

Ho, H. et al. (2016) The effect of oat ß-glucan on LDL-cholesterol, non-HDL-cholesterol and apoB for CVD risk reduction: a systematic review and meta-analysis of randomised-controlled trials. [Accessed: March 2024 via https://pubmed.ncbi.nlm.nih.gov/27724985/]

Longo, V., and Mattson, M. (2014) Fasting: Molecular Mechanisms and Clinical Applications. [Accessed: March 2024 via https://www.ncbi.nlm.nih.gov/pmc/articles/PMC3946160/]

McDonald, D., et al. (2018) American Gut: an Open Platform for Citizen Science Microbiome Research. [Accessed: March 2024 via https://doi.org/10.1128/msystems.00031-18]

Moustarah, F., and Daley, S. (2024) Dietary Iron [Accessed: March 2024 via https://www.ncbi.nlm.nih.gov/books/NBK540969/]

Rodgers, B., Kirley, K., and Mounsey, A. (2013) Prescribing an antibiotic? Pair it with probiotics [Accessed: March 2024 via https://www.ncbi.nlm.nih.gov/pmc/articles/PMC3601687/]

Wiertsema., S., et al. (2021) The Interplay between the Gut Microbiome and the Immune System in the Context of Infectious Diseases throughout Life and the Role of Nutrition in Optimizing Treatment Strategies [Accessed: March 2024 via https://www.ncbi.nlm.nih.gov/pmc/articles/PMC8001875/]

CHAPTER 7

BDA Fat Fact Sheet (2021) [Accessed: March 2024 via https://www.bda.uk.com/resource/fat.html]

Leeuwendaal, N., et al. (2022) Fermented Foods, Health and the Gut Microbiome. Nutrients. [Accessed: March 2024 via https://doi.org/10.3390/nu14050921]

Mayer, E., et al. (2014) Gut Microbes and the Brain: paradigm shift in neuroscience. Journal of Neuroscience [Accessed: March 2024 via https://www.ncbi.nlm.nih.gov/pmc/articles/PMC4228144/]

CHAPTER 8

Fujiwara, Y., et al. (2005) Association Between Dinner-to-Bed Time and Gastro-Esophageal Reflux Disease. [Accessed: March 2024 via https://pubmed.ncbi.nlm.nih.gov/16393212/]

Pipoyan, D., et al. (2021) The Effect of Trans Fatty Acids on Human Health. PMC. [Accessed: March 2024 via https://www.ncbi.nlm.nih.gov/pmc/articles/PMC8535577/]

Robinson, E., et al. (2013) Eating attentively: a systematic review and meta-analysis of the effect of food intake memory and awareness on eating. American Journal of Clinical Nutrition, [Accessed: March 2024 https://doi.org/10.3945/ajcn.112.045245]

St-Onge, M-P., et al. (2016) Effects of Diet on Sleep Quality. Advances in Nutrition [Accessed: March 2024 via https://www.ncbi.nlm.nih.gov/pmc/articles/PMC5015038/]

Zelman, K. (n.d.) Slow down, you eat too fast. [Accessed: March 2024 via https://www.webmd.com/obesity/features/slow-down-you-eat-too-fast]

ACKNOWLEDGEMENTS

I would firstly like to thank and acknowledge Ru Merritt for trusting me to write this book and for providing such incredibly valuable feedback during the editing process. This book would not be here if it wasn't for you! Thank you to the whole team at Penguin Random House including Jasleen, Kate and Beth for your help and support, and to Joe, Ellie and Megan on the photography team, too. I would also like to thank Melissa Kuman (Registered Nutritionist) for helping me to research this book, and Helen West (Registered Dietitian) for peer reviewing the manuscript – your insight, wisdom and knowledge are much appreciated. Thank you to Dr Frankie Phillips and Maeve Hanan (Registered Dietitians) for answering my many questions and thank you to Sophie Knoxx (Associate Nutritionist) for providing guidance on many of the healthy recipes contained within this book.

A special thank you to my husband Oliver and my parents Maggie and Phil, without whom I would have not have been afforded the time to write this book. From supporting with childcare to recipe testing, thank you for putting up with the many late nights and weekends at my laptop. I appreciate all of you so much. Thank you for the constant motivation and for believing in me, always.

And thank you to you, the reader, for picking up this book. I really hope it has helped or inspired you in some way. Let me know how you get on by tagging me on social media @nicsnutrition.

I would like to end by acknowledging the author Dr Chris van Tulleken, for bringing the topic of UPFs into the public eye and mainstream media.

ABOUT THE AUTHOR

A passionate and trusted voice, **Nichola Ludlam-Raine (BSc hons, PG Dip, MSc)** is a specialist Registered Dietitian with over fifteen years of clinical experience working for the NHS as well as privately. She shares inspiring content to over 100,000 followers on social media (follow her at @nicsnutrition and @mummynutrition), has appeared on TV numerous times – Nichola is a regular on BBC Breakfast, ITV Tonight, Channel 4 and Channel 5 – and regularly provides commentary to numerous tabloids and press outlets. She advocates for a better relationship with food, so that others can build healthier habits that lead to lasting change.